Created in God's Image: Meditating on Our Body

by
Carl Koch and Joyce Heil

Saint Mary's Press
Christian Brothers Publications
Winona, Minnesota

℘ Dedications ℘

To Vondell, Jeff, and Keung,
for the gift of your profound and faithful friendship.
—Carl

To Mom and Dad,
my Franciscan Sisters of Perpetual Adoration,
and my friends,
all of whom have helped me appreciate the gift of myself.
—Joyce

The publishing team for this book included Stephan Nagel, development editor; Barbara Bartelson, typesetter; and Elaine Kohner, illustrator.

The acknowledgments continue on page 120.

Printed in the United States of America

Printing: 6 5 4 3 2 1

Year: 1997 96 95 94 93 92 91

ISBN 0-88489-251-4

Contents

Preface   7

Introduction   10

Meditations

1. **Appraising Our Body Image**   15

2. **Telling Our Body's Story**   20

3. **Our Most Sensational Organ: The Skin**   26

4. **Made for Motion: Our Feet and Legs**   31

5. **Deliberate Extensions: Our Arms and Hands**   36

6. **Tough and Tender: Our Torso**   41

7. **Under the Fig Leaf: The Male Sexual Organs**   46

8. **Form Follows Function: The Female Sexual Organs**   51

9. **Working Partners: Our Bones and Muscles**   56

10. **The Heart of the Matter: Our Heart and Circulation**   62

11. **The Breath of Life: Our Lungs**   67

12. **The Outside In: Our Digestive System**   72

13. **The Gunpowder Trail: Our Nervous System**   78

14. **Who Knows? Our Nose**   84

15. **Camera and Computer: Our Eyes**   88

16. **The Sound and the Swing: Our Ears**   93

17. **Chat and Chew: Our Mouth**   98

18. **Data and Dreams: Our Brain**   103

19. **Affirming Our Body**   108

20. **Nurturing Our Body**   113

Appendix   117

Created in God's Image

Endorsements for
Created in God's Image:
Meditating on Our Body

"We live in an era that might be earmarked as having three descriptive characteristics. It is an age of unprecedented physical violence, a time of relentless noise
and hype, a time when the place of prayer in human life is set aside in the name of
personal rights granted through amendments to our nation's documents. This
book has the potential to serve as an antidote to all three with its affirming and
healing approach to the body, in its invitation to the kind of solitude that invites
one to seek quiet and personal reflection, and in its reminders of the important
place of prayer in every person's life."
—**Paula Ripple,** former executive director of the North American Conference of
Separated and Divorced Catholics; author of *Growing Strong at Broken Places*

కం

"Suspicion and outright condemnation of the human body have haunted
Christian spirituality for much of its history. For those of us raised with such
attitudes, *Created in God's Image* is a realistic and practical guide for befriending
the gift of our bodiliness. It contains insightful medical information and
theological reflections, as well as helpful meditative exercises, drawings, and
prayers. Koch's and Heil's book is truly a celebration of the wonder and wisdom
of human flesh, bones, and heart."
—**Edward C. Sellner,** PhD, associate professor of pastoral theology and spirituality, College of Saint Catherine, Saint Paul, MN; author of *Soul-Making: The
Telling of a Spiritual Journey*

కం

"A much-needed resource for Christian meditation on the wonders of creation in
the body. *Created in God's Image* combines traditional anatomy and physiology
with suggestions for prayerful reflection designed to heal our relationship to body
image, self-esteem, sexuality, and the whole range of being human in an embodied
way. This book opens a new arena for Christian thought and praxis. *Created in
God's Image* counteracts centuries of scripture interpretations that denigrate the
sacred temple of the body. As the great mystics and prophets of the Judeo-
Christian-Islamic tradition have known and taught, the essence of divine life is to
be found mirrored in each blade of grass and each wrinkle of skin—in the
compassionate warp and weft of the whole universe of creation."
—**Neil Douglas-Klotz,** instructor in Body Prayer and Dances of Universal Peace,
Institute of Culture and Creation Spirituality, Holy Names College; author of
Prayers of the Cosmos

Preface

I spent most Sundays during September and October of 1989 visiting a wonderful friend who was in treatment for an addiction to diet pills and alcohol. In her early forties, she had just started coming to terms with the trauma of the sexual abuse perpetrated upon her by an older adult relative from the time she was four until she turned twelve. I found these visits both inspiring and frustrating. The visits inspired me because my friend was coming to grips with and recovering from a trauma that had been repressed for nearly thirty years and had shaped her life in some distinctly unhealthy ways. She showed more courage and hope than I have ever found in myself.

My frustration grew because her loathing for her body and the destruction of her self-esteem left her nearly incapable of affirming her physical beauty or her value as a person. Indeed, her physical beauty had become her enemy; she had learned to equate beauty with attracting her abuser. Thus, when she was a small child, her instinct for survival told her to get fat. Fat would repel her abuser. Fatness did not prevent the abuse, of course; it only established a pattern of overeating.

During adolescence, being overweight became a liability. She sought help from diet pills and lost weight. Then people began to compliment her about how good she looked. These compliments, especially from men, triggered her old fears, and my friend became caught in a vicious cycle of diets and weight gain. She not only suffered shame from being abused but also from being overweight and addicted. Overcoming so much shame and self-loathing will be a lifelong project, but as she recovers, she can believe and accept tiny bits of affirmation. A loving embrace of herself remains a distant goal.

During these months of companioning my friend in recovery, I thought long and hard about ways in which I might help nourish her self-esteem. Naturally I brought these concerns to my spiritual director, a wise woman. I remember railing at the Church's history of teaching suspicion and even denigration of the body, and I stated that nothing had been written to help Christians enjoy, appreciate, and embrace their bodiliness. Mary Kathryn smiled calmly and said, "Well, you're a writer."

I had to consider this challenge at great length before I finally embarked on the project. I did have a personal incentive. I have been attempting to change from old habits of compulsive eating. Through the guidance of a nutritionist, exercise, and regular recourse to prayer, I have begun a path to wellness. But I am still learning to cherish, appreciate, and take care of my body. Years of obesity taught me to be ashamed of it. Paradoxically, however, my own recovery only began when I woke up and realized that I liked myself better than I ever had and did not want to kill myself with fat or let fat prevent me from doing all the things I would like to do.

The shame I experience from being obese cannot compare with the shame and guilt my friend has experienced as an incest survivor. However, in our own way, we each need to learn a love for the body that God has created for us. As whole human beings—body and spirit—we cannot love ourselves fully until we learn to love our body. So this book is intended to help those of us who have treated our body as an enemy or, at least, have been too ashamed of it to appreciate, value, and nurture it as a loved part of our self. People who already find comfort and joy with their body can anticipate finding additional sources of wonder and celebration.

When I decided to take on this project, I recognized right away that I would need expert help from a woman coauthor. I might understand something of the male experience of bodiliness, but I do not have the temerity to claim much understanding of the female experience. In addition, my coauthor would need a thorough knowledge of anatomy and physiology. By fortunate chance, a friend suggested that I contact Joyce Heil. With her background in nursing and teaching, and with her training in spirituality, Joyce has certainly been the perfect partner. Besides, she possesses the sense of humor necessary to write meditations on such atypical topics as the digestive tract and the inner ear.

Joyce and I would like to thank our many generous and wise consultants: Maureen Schaukowitch, OSF; Barbara Kole, FMDM; Lee Wilson; Armand Alcazar, FSC; Bob Fagan, FSC; Mary Lu Kugel;

Lou Anne Tighe; Joan Maresh; and Mary Kathryn Fogarty, FSPA (who is also my spiritual director).

May this book help to bring joy, health, wonder, and songs of praise of the Creator to all who read it and meditate with it.

CARL KOCH, FSC

Introduction

The Purpose of This Book

This book can serve to praise and glorify God by helping us encounter the Creator in a unique creation—our body. By valuing our body, we can build the temple of God. By loving ourself, we can be empowered to love other people.

Many of us have been convinced that our body is ugly or at least inadequate. Television advertisements scream at us to buy products that will hide our blemishes, pull in our sagging waistline, firm up our breasts, and make us smell seductive or "manly." Advertisers do not want us to feel good about our body. If we did, we might not feel a need to buy their wares. The meditations in this book can help us examine the negative messages that we have received about our body and begin the self-healing process.

Besides suffering from the visual and verbal assault by advertisers, many men and women have suffered abuse by other people. Survivors of sexual abuse and those who have lived through the nightmare of physical or emotional abuse often have difficulty cherishing their bodies. Hopefully, these meditations will help all of us to accept our body as a gift and to heal any memories of abuse or misuse.

By meditating on our body, we might become aware of ways in which we can nurture and enjoy our body more wholly. One way of praising and thanking someone who gives us a gift is to use the gift well. For instance, if a relative gives you a shirt for your birthday, you can show that you value both the gift and the giver by wearing, taking care of, and enjoying it. We can thank and praise God for our body by using, nurturing, and enjoying it.

The meditations invite you to experience your body in new, affirming ways. We develop a more positive, godlike way of imaging our body not by intellect alone, but more so through experiencing the wonder of our body—which the meditations help us do. **Each meditation has more reflection activities than can be done during one prayer period. Therefore, select only one or two reflection activities each time you use a meditation. Do not feel compelled to complete all of the reflection activities. If you are unfamiliar with the different styles of meditating that are suggested in the reflection activities, you may wish to read the appendix found on pages 117–119.**

Give yourself a break. Enter into the experience of the meditations patiently, with an open mind, a generous spirit, and a willing body. Give yourself time to get used to the idea that you are made in God's image. After all, we are not told this truth very often. It's a realization that takes growing into.

Made in God's Image

All human beings are made in God's image.

> God said, "Let us make human beings in our own image, in the likeness of ourselves." . . . God created human beings in God's own image, in the image of God they were created, male and female God created them. . . . God blessed them. . . . And so it was, looking at all of Creation, God recognized it as very good. (Adapted from Genesis 1:26–31)

Granted, God does not have a personal body, so humans were created to reflect the power, wonder, and mystery of the Creator. All human beings—no matter how short or tall, fat or thin, disfigured or unblemished, athletic or sedentary—are made in the image of their Creator, the one perfect God.

Obvious? Maybe not. After all, if we human beings genuinely believed ourselves to be made in God's image and likeness, would we flirt with skin cancer by over-sunning ourselves? Would we wear clothing that squeezes us and shoes that crimp? Would we pay billions of dollars for diets that usually end in frustration and binges?

When we like ourself, warts and all, we dance instead of standing around. We walk proud and free instead of shuffling along slump-shouldered. We glow with confidence.

Trouble in Paradise

None of us would accuse the Creator of lying in proclaiming that human beings were made in God's image. Nevertheless, we may have a difficult time believing this—as did Adam and Eve, in the story of Creation. Indeed, Adam and Eve banished themselves from Paradise because they could not believe that they were made in the likeness of their Creator.

Recall the story of the Fall. God gives Adam and Eve the garden of Eden—a paradise—in which to live. Only one thing is forbidden: they must not eat from the tree of the knowledge of good and evil.

Naturally, the tempter arrives in the garden, knowing the one argument with which to lure Adam and Eve to eat from the forbidden tree. The serpent says, "God knows that when you eat from this tree, your eyes will be opened and you will be like gods." In other words, the serpent knows Adam and Eve do not truly believe themselves to already be made in the image and likeness of God. The serpent is right; they eat of the forbidden fruit, hoping to become like gods. You know the rest of the story.

We are made wonderfully godlike. If we believe and accept this truth, we can bask in the beauty of God's creation. When we see as the Creator sees, creation manifests all its glory. One of the Creator's glories is our body. When we nurture and delight in our body, when we use it for the good of humankind, we co-create with God. We build the new Eden that comes with the Reign of God.

The Word Becomes Flesh

The all-merciful God liberated us from the Fall. God chose to bring salvation through Jesus, who did not spurn bodiliness, even death of the body. Jesus chose to become a human being. And so "the Word became flesh, / he lived among us" (John 1:14). Jesus was "in every way like a human being / . . . even to accepting death" and "did not count equality with God / something to be grasped" (Philippians 2:7–8,6).

In other words, by becoming fully human, Jesus showed us that we human beings are lovable and are made in God's image and likeness—in body, mind, and spirit. Jesus is the new Adam, believing in the goodness of humanity and affirming that to be fully human is to grow in our godlikeness. Even after his death and resurrection, Jesus did not spurn his body but ascended in it.

Temples of God

When Saint Paul admonishes the Corinthians for misusing their bodies through incest, ritual prostitution, and other dehumanizing acts, he writes to them: "Do you not realise that you are a temple of God with the Spirit of God living in you? . . . God's temple is holy; and you are that temple" (1 Corinthians 3:16–17). Even though Jesus showed us the goodness of our humanity, the temptations to degrade it continually beckon. In many cases, we simply have never learned to celebrate and build "our temple."

From a Christian point of view, our body is a temple of God. Nurturing our body and employing our body for loving service become ways of worshiping God.

Considered in another light, how can we be followers of Jesus in our world if we do not treat our body reverently? Our body, like the body of Jesus, is the means by which we reach out to other people, feed the hungry, clothe the naked, visit the sick, and shelter the homeless. With our hands, our eyes, and our voices, we caress the ones we love. Our eyes study the word of God, and our ears listen to the voice of God. Our blessed body mediates the love of God to other people.

God's Artwork

Another statement by Saint Paul provides still a different image of the wonder of our humanity. He tells the Ephesians: "We are God's work of art, created in Christ Jesus for the good works which God has already designated to make up our way of life" (Ephesians 2:10). We are works of art that only the Supreme Artist could create. But God does not make art for art's sake. We are created for good works. We are invited to reverence our body, not just because it is wonderfully, beautifully made, but also because we need it to live the full life of service to which Jesus calls us.

We are artworks, but we are also artists. We help shape each other and ourselves. We can build up or we can tear down. Recall ways you build yourself up. Maybe you swim or walk. Perhaps you thank God for being able to dance or to work with your hands.

Remember statements that have torn you down—the times, for instance, when you have looked in the mirror and said things like "I hate my nose." Jesus urges us to be artists who build up.

Finally, to be fully valued, a work of art must be viewed by someone who knows enough about art to appreciate it. To value our bodiliness—the work of art that we are—takes time and some knowledge. The promise in Saint Paul's words is that in appreciating ourself as a work of art, we will also appreciate and praise the Creator, the God who formed us.

Before You Begin

May this book be a healing and hopeful journey for you. . . .
We are created in God's image,
Temples of God,
God's works of art.
Amen. Alleluia!

Meditation 1

Appraising Our Body Image

Opening prayer: God our creator, free my perception to see your image in myself.

Wondrous Facts

Human bodies come in all shapes, sizes, and colors. Each is unique and wonderful—formed by both heredity and environment. By pondering the uncontrollable yet wise forces that have shaped our body, we can cherish it better.

Consider, for instance, the three major human body types—Negroid, Mongoloid, and Caucasoid. Each of these body types is the result of millennia of adaptations to the requirements for survival in a particular climate.

These adaptations are most dramatic where climates reach extremes. The stocky stature of the Inuit people, or Eskimos, suits them well for the Arctic climate, where exposure kills quickly. Their compact body size yields a low body surface area relative to volume, and their short limbs ensure that blood flows efficiently to their extremities. Increased blood flow and a heavier-than-average fat layer help to protect them from frostbite. Also, researchers find that the Eskimo's metabolism is 15 to 30 percent higher than the European's. People native to tropical climates tend to have leaner bodies, with more surface area in relation to their weight. This build provides an increased exposure of skin to the air so that evaporation may take place, thus cooling the body.

Our racial origins clearly have a central role in giving us our particular body. On a more personal level, our family traits account for our looks. From the moment of our birth, people may have said how much we resemble our mother or father. We are a unique combination of the genes of our parents, but a combination nonetheless. Not too many centers on basketball teams are the offspring of short, stocky parents.

With all our racial differences, however, we share almost all the same genes and ultimately descend from the same ancestors—simpler creatures whose nonhuman features we still exhibit in our embryonic stage. All human embryos, for example, have tiny tails that disappear before birth, although very infrequently a child is born with a tail that must be removed surgically. Likewise, six months before birth, the human fetus is covered with a layer of downy fur called lanugo. This also vanishes before birth.

In assessing our body image, therefore, bringing to mind some of the ways in which our body has been formed by external, uncontrollable forces may help us to acknowledge and appreciate the power of God in shaping our life and the lives of others.

Reflection

Our body results from an awesome mixture of ancestral and environmental forces. Our body image—the way we perceive our body—results from millions of bits of information that we gather from events, relationships with people, work and leisure activities, the media, and so on. Everything that happens contributes to the sense we have of our bodiliness. Some people give us positive messages about our body; other people send us negative messages. All these bits of information help compose our body image, but over forming this image we do have some control.

God would have us see our body for what it is—a gracious, wonderful gift, made in God's image. Yet the body remembers. Negative messages about our body received as a toddler may later result in severe anxiety, eating disorders, stomach ulcers, or other dysfunctions. Positive messages are remembered too and can manifest themselves in fine posture, glowing skin, bright eyes, and a dynamic presence.

This book of meditations about your body begins with a meditation designed to help you assess your body image. How do you feel about your body? How aware are you of your body image? Assessing our body may be like describing the proverbial glass of water: an optimist sees a half-full glass; a pessimist sees a half-empty glass. Some of us see our body as "half-full"; others, as "half-empty." This meditation can help you size up your body image.

✥ Relax your body by slowly tensing and relaxing each part. Start with your feet. Tense and relax them. Then your legs, and so on, until you have relaxed your entire body. Go slowly.

Close your eyes and get in touch with how you are experiencing your body right now. How do you feel about your body? Make a mental tour of your body from top to bottom to inventory your feelings.

When you have finished this "feelings inventory," spend some time writing down your feelings. List them in any order. Then try to write a summary of your feelings.

✥ Slow down. Sit comfortably but alertly, perhaps with your back straight, feet on the floor, and hands resting in your lap. Breathe deeply and slowly for several minutes. Relax yourself by closing your eyes and concentrating on your deep breathing.

Imagine that you are at a party or gathering. Someone whom you admire greatly is there. You have never met this person, but have always wanted to. This person sees you and comes toward you from across the room. As the person comes toward you, what do you feel he or she is thinking about your body? How do you feel about your body in the presence of this person?

Ponder, perhaps in writing, what your reactions during this meditation exercise say about your own body image.

✍ Relax your body. Tense your muscles and relax them. Begin with your feet and tense and relax all the way to your face.

When you are relaxed—open to your body and to the Spirit in you—think about the one aspect of your body that you most dislike, or have felt uncomfortable or embarrassed about.

If possible, examine this part of your body, directly or by using a mirror. What is it that most disturbs you about this body part? What experiences have caused you to feel the way you do?

Next, write a dialog between you and the body part that most annoys you. At first you may feel silly doing this exercise, but give it a chance. Say what you want to the part and ask it questions. Then, let the part speak back. You might just make some new discoveries in the dialog process.

When you and your body part have finished exchanging views, read over the dialog. Did you learn anything about your body image or your behavior toward your body?

Spend some time talking to the Creator about your interaction with the part of you that has become a source of disturbance.

✍ Position yourself before a mirror, preferably one that allows you to see your entire body. Slowly pray the following litany. As you do, look at the part of your body about which you are praying.

- Gracious God, thank you for the gift of my skin.
- I thank you, Creator God, for my feet and legs.
- For my arms and hands, I give thanks to you, God.
- Source of life and all delight, I thank you for my chest and abdomen.
- Giver of my life, thank you for my sexual organs.
- For my bones and muscles, I give you thanks.
- Lungs and heart you have given me. Thank you, good God.
- Creator God, for my digestive system, thanks.
- I give you thanks for my nervous system.
- For my nose, eyes, ears, mouth, and voice, I give you thanks.
- Loving God, thank you for my brain.

✦ God, you created me in your image and likeness. I give you thanks for the miracle of my body, for all of me.

Conclude your litany-meditation by caressing and admiring your body with your eyes. Then, in writing or by speaking out loud, express your reactions to the litany-meditation in the form of a prayer to God, who created you.

God's Word

Yahweh, you search me and know me.
You know if I am standing or sitting.
You perceive my thoughts from far away.
Whether I walk or lie down, you are watching;
you are familiar with all my ways.
You created my inmost being
and knit me together in my mother's womb.
For all these mysteries—
for the wonder of myself,
for the wonder of your works—
I thank you.

(Psalm 139:1–3,13–14)

Closing prayer: I am created in God's image. For the wonder of myself, I thank you, loving God.

Meditation 2

Telling Our Body's Story

Opening prayer: Loving God, as I become more aware of the story of my body, may I also become more aware of your creative power in my life.

Wondrous Facts

The story of our body stretches back to before recorded history. The human body is a result both of environmental forces and of the ancestors who adapted to those forces. The human species retained those physical characteristics that aided in survival, and generally failed to pass on those that did not. This process continues within our species, but so slowly that we cannot discern it.

Our body gives us hints to our particular family's "body story." If you have good eyes or teeth, outstanding athletic ability, keen intelligence, a strong heart, or thick hair, chances are that so do your parents and grandparents. But everyone alive today can claim lineage from vigorous, hardy people who survived all sorts of dangers and diseases. One of our great ancestral gifts is our body's automatic response to emergencies. Stress of any kind throws the body into an intricate, total response—psychological and physiological. In a full stress response, the autonomic, or involuntary, nervous system prepares the body to deal with stress. Adrenaline production increases, blood pressure and blood sugar levels rise, and the heart and respiratory rates quicken, bringing an increase of oxygen to the muscles. The pupils dilate, and the hands and feet sweat. Digestion decreases so that more blood may flow to the brain, heart, and muscles. The body acts as a powerful, unified force intent on survival.

On the other hand, predispositions to certain illnesses can also originate in our familial past. A genetic predisposition means that an abnormal gene exists within the reproductive pool and may be transferred to the offspring. For example, diabetes and epilepsy may be inherited. Other conditions and diseases also tend to run in families: scoliosis (also known as "curvature of the spine"), high blood pressure, and obesity are examples of conditions that tend to be passed along through generations, though in some cases the environment plays as important a role as heredity.

Environment, like evolution, can be a "telling" force—both positive and negative—in the story of our body. In a nurturing family, for instance, members are inclined to be stable, balanced, and caring people. However, certain illnesses also have their origins in environmental sources: some cancers, nervous disorders, and even eating dysfunctions can have causes in our surroundings.

We are largely products of the story of our body, and many of our attitudes about our body derive from family training and education. The remaining element of our story line is our personal environment—that is, the things that we have changed in ourself and our surroundings through our own decisions and accomplishments. Perhaps we are involved in activities that are unusual for our family, like being the first member to run cross country in high school or to attend college. Or maybe we have taken on disciplines regarding diet that differ from our family's habits. A good first step toward shaping our own story is to learn about it: the more we know about our body, the more we can value it as a source of wonder at how God creates and how we can co-create.

Reflection

When doctors do complete physical examinations, they frequently ask patients to give them a medical history. Most often, the checklist includes items like illnesses, accidents, surgeries, incidence of mental illness in the family, and so on. With this history, doctors can look for any possible effects of past illnesses or genetic predispositions. Doing this type of body history is valuable.

However, our body's story also includes the mastery of physical skills or creative abilities, and the positive care with which we have nurtured our body.

Meditating on our body's story can help us become aware of the body we have and what has affected it over the years. Meditation may also lead to new awareness of hidden feelings—fears and joys—connected with events in our story. This awareness can lead to celebration and healing.

Write about the most important events in your body's story. Begin with the first important event in your body's story and continue to the present. You might want to chart your story in three columns:

* In column 1, write down the year.
* In column 2, write a brief description of the important event, for example, undergoing eye surgery, winning a track meet, or breaking a finger.
* In column 3, describe the physical and emotional effects that you underwent at the time and over the long run. For example, eye surgery can bring with it a fear of blindness, sensitivity to the unsighted, trouble driving, self-consciousness, or a new appreciation for colors.

After describing the story of your body, select the one point of your body's story that is most important to you. Spend some time writing about why this event has so much significance. How has this event shaped your attitude about your body and about yourself as a whole? What have been the long-range effects of this event?

Has your body's story influenced the ways in which you have related to God? Dialog with God about this question.

You have done a story of your body, but many physical aspects of our body are inherited.

- List the parts of your body and, next to each one, try to identify the family member from whom you might have inherited its characteristics.
- Then list the names of your grandparents and parents. After each name, describe that person's general health and list the diseases or illnesses from which he or she suffered.

What attitudes toward illness have you learned from your family? Which of these attitudes are healthy? Are any of them unhealthy?

If possible, find a picture that includes all the members of your immediate family. Even better, try to find family portraits from your childhood, adolescence, and young adulthood. If you cannot find a picture, close your eyes and compose a picture of your immediate family in your mind.

Study each picture. Were members of your family pleased with the body that God gave them? Who liked their body and who did not? For each person, try to remember particular examples that demonstrated their liking or disliking for their body.

Among your family members, who was most influential in the formation of your attitudes about your body? Was what you learned from this person about your body mostly positive, or was it negative? Are you still holding on to what this person taught you?

Write a list of the parts of your body with which you presently feel comfortable or parts that you actually like, and explain why you like each part.

Then, next to each part of your body that you like, write the names of people, advertisements, media images, or other influences that helped you to like this aspect of your body.

Now, list the parts of your body with which you feel uncomfortable or parts that you dislike, and list the reasons why.

Next to each part you do not like, write the names of people, advertisements, media images, or other influences that gave you reasons to dislike this part.

Finally, record what you have learned about your body—both positive and negative—and ask yourself: "What do I want to feel about my body now? How can I let go of the negative attitudes? Would the Creator want me to feel negatively about myself?"

❧ Bring to mind the person who has had the most negative impact on your body image. You may need to do some brainstorming during which you draw up several names and then pick the name of the one person who has most hurt your body image.

Now, close your eyes, relax your entire body, and concentrate on your breathing.

Imagine that you are talking to this person with Jesus present during the conversation. If you would prefer a woman's presence, invite Mary, Mary Magdalene, Julian of Norwich, or another supportive, holy woman to accompany you. Explain how this individual hurt your body image. Do not hold anything back, resentments and anger, questions and frustrations. Then, imagine this person's response. Listen carefully to what this person says. Finally, let Jesus, or your female companion, talk to both of you. What would Jesus or your female companion say to heal you?

If you find this process helpful, repeat it with the other people who have hurt you in the past and with whom you would like to experience a healing of these hurts.

❧ Recall the people who have been most affirming to your body image. Pick the one person who has most helped you accept the gift of your body.

Close your eyes, breathe deeply, and relax.

Imagine that this positive person and Jesus are with you right now. Let this friend act in the manner that you find so affirming to your body image. Express your gratitude to this person. Then imagine what Jesus would say to the two of you.

If you feel comfortable doing so, call or write to this affirming person, expressing your thanks for the ways in which she or he has helped you over the years.

Finally, if this meditation activity has been helpful, repeat it with other supportive people whom you recall.

❧ Describe the ways in which your job or home influence your bodily well-being, both positively and negatively. Describe such things as physical or emotional stresses (for example, fumes, mechanical hazards, poor lighting, noises, and relationships that cause conflict) and constructive or supportive conditions and co-workers.

God's Word

Better be poor if healthy and fit
>than rich if tormented in body.
Health and strength are better than any gold,
>a robust body than untold wealth.
No riches can outweigh bodily health,
>no enjoyment surpass a cheerful heart. . . .
Do not abandon yourself to sorrow,
>do not torment yourself with brooding.
Gladness of heart is life to anyone,
>joy is what gives length of days.
Give your cares the slip, console your heart,
>chase sorrow far away;
for sorrow has been the ruin of many,
>and is no use to anybody.
Jealousy and anger shorten your days,
>and worry brings premature old age.

>(Ecclesiasticus 30:14–16,21–24)

Closing prayer: God, my creator, grant me a genial heart and a positive love of my entire self—body and spirit. May I embrace the story of my body, heal the wounds, celebrate the joys, and begin a new and more wonderful chapter in my story.

Meditation 3

Our Most Sensational Organ: The Skin

Opening prayer: You are present now, God, my friend. You created my skin, a genuine wonder. May it glow with love for you and the world you made.

Wondrous Facts

Covering approximately eighteen and a half square feet and weighing about six pounds in adults, the skin is the largest organ of our body. This waterproof and protective covering keeps the internal environment of the body intact and ensures that life is possible.

Besides covering our body, the skin fulfills other essential functions, such as secretion, sensation, heat regulation, and the production of essential chemicals for the body.

Our skin regulates body temperature by secreting sweat. The moisture evaporates, thus cooling us. We have around three million sweat glands. During a summer day, our sweat glands can easily lose up to two quarts of fluid. On a really torrid day, we can sweat over two gallons. In humid climates, sweat cannot evaporate efficiently, but just oozes out, not cooling the body.

The blood vessels in our skin trigger the sweating process. In hot weather, these blood vessels send more blood to our skin to push the heat outward. Our skin reddens. When we are cold, we appear pale because our body sends less blood to the skin, in order to conserve heat inside.

Sensation is one of the most important functions of our skin. Besides containing receptors for sensing temperature, fine touch, pressure, and joint position, the skin also produces millions of hair follicles and their nerve endings, which are among the body's most sensitive touch-end organs. The surface of the body varies greatly in the distribution of these sensory receptors. For instance, if you took two ballpoint pens and touched their tips to your finger, with only one-tenth of an inch separating the tips, you could distinguish sensation at two points. However, if you touched the tips of the pens to your thigh, the distance required to detect that there were two tips and not one would have to be three inches. (Try this.)

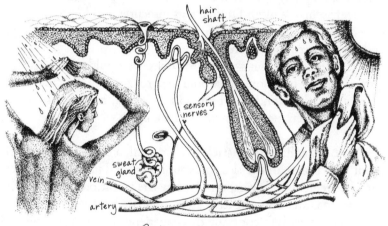

Systems in our skin

Our skin also manufactures wonderful chemicals. When you sustain a cut, your skin and your blood immediately start the healing process. Blood forms clots, and special glands in your skin release an antiseptic fluid to eliminate germs. Skin color comes from a pigment called melanin, which is also manufactured by the skin. This pigment prevents harmful ultraviolet rays of sunlight from penetrating the skin. Increased exposure to sunlight stimulates growth of skin that is thicker and darker, accounting for the variation of skin colors throughout the world.

Finally, our wondrous skin is a constantly renewing resource. Layers of dead skin are continually being shed to be replaced with new layers. One estimate is that every day ten billion bits of skin flake off. In a lifetime we may shed over forty pounds of skin. Think about it—part of your past gets sucked into your vacuum each time you clean your carpet!

Reflection

Besides doing all the wonderful and essential things it does for our body, the skin defines our appearance in many ways. Aspects of our identity include the color of our hair, the shape of our ears, the smoothness of our face, or the wrinkles on our forehead.

Advertisers certainly recognize the importance of the skin in the makeup of our identity. Perhaps the majority of body-care products advertised are intended for our skin—shampoos, deodorants, colognes, soaps, lotions, creams, salves, and so on. In almost all cases, advertisements intend to make us insecure: our skin is either too pale or the wrong color, too wrinkled or too dry. Our hair has split ends, is too frizzy, or does not bounce.

If we looked at our skin as God does, we would see a wonder of form matching function. We would seek to care for our skin because it is part of the wonderful body God gave us, not because it is a wretched burden meant to make us look ugly.

🖎 With a small, smooth stick like a pencil, a chopstick, or a ballpoint pen, touch all the skin on your hands and forearms. Run the stick between your fingers, too. Notice the variations in sensitivity. Which areas are most sensitive and which are least sensitive?

You may wish to continue this experience by touching the stick to other areas of your body. This activity helps us appreciate the marvelous matching of sensitivity to function of parts of our skin. Take your time doing this exploration, and remember the giver of this gift.

🖎 Take a slow bath or shower. Pay attention to your skin. As you feel the water pouring over you, reflect upon the ways in which your skin is

protecting you . . .
regulating your body temperature . . .
sending messages to your mind . . .

𝓟𝒶 Lie down on the floor. Close your eyes, and breathe slowly and deeply for a few moments. Then concentrate your attention on the feelings where your body is touching the floor—your heels, calves, thighs, buttocks, back, arms, and head. How does the floor feel? Hard or soft? Cool or warm? Rough or smooth? Be open to all the subtle differences of feeling.

Turn on your side or front. Notice the parts of your body touching the floor. Focus again on all the sensations you are experiencing.

𝓟𝒶 Go for a walk outdoors. Pay attention to the sensations that you feel on your skin. Notice the feelings caused by the texture and weight of your clothes and shoes. How do these sensations make you feel all over? Conclude your walk by conversing with God about this experience.

𝓟𝒶 Our aging manifests itself earliest on our skin and in our hair. Wrinkles and graying hair can be viewed as badges of wisdom and experience, or as signs of demise. Take a good look at your wrinkles. Can you accept them, even embrace them, as part of your growth and beauty? Try affirming these wrinkles and gray hairs as part of your maturity.

𝓟𝒶 Do a scar-search. Most of us have scars, the results of injury or surgery. Look at each of your scars and recall the cause of each one. Reflect on the healing process that followed. Did you ever thank your skin for the healing, or celebrate the miracle of regeneration with the Supreme Healer?

𝓟𝒶 Do you have any negative experiences related to your skin in your story? Review these and then, one by one, let go of them. You may wish to say something like, "I let go of this [name the negative experience]. I don't need it any more."

𝓟𝒶 Check out your medicine chest: What sort of salves and creams do you use on your skin? Why? Do they really help, or do you just hope that they will? How about soap and shampoo? Why do you select the ones that you use? Are they actually helpful for your skin?

After considering the products that you use on your skin, reflect on, and perhaps write responses to, these questions:

◆ What attitudes do I have toward my skin?

+ Is my skin an adversary that shows my age, or is it a friend that is simply part of who I am?

❀ What is your attitude toward sweat? Do you experience it as a friend or as an enemy? Is most of what you hear about perspiration positive, or is it negative? Ponder the importance of sweat. People without sweat glands must live their entire lives in a totally climate-controlled environment. Could you feel better about the gift of sweat?

❀ Consider going for a massage from a trained, licensed massage therapist. This is one good way of nurturing not only your skin, but your whole body-spirit.

❀ Slowly read "God's Word" found below. Doesn't our skin radiate what is going on inside? When we are embarrassed, for instance, our face brightens. Write a dialog between you and your skin; discuss the state of your inner life. Does the God who loves you shine forth in the skin of your face—no matter if it is freckled or plain, wrinkled or smooth, leathery or soft? Or do people see a dullness there because you have not opened yourself to the love that God has for you?

God's Word

> When Moses came down from Mount Sinai with the two tablets of the Testimony in his hands, as he was coming down the mountain, Moses did not know that the skin of his face was radiant because he had been talking to [God]. And when Aaron and all the Israelites saw Moses, the skin on his face was so radiant that they were afraid to go near him. But Moses called to them. . . . (Exodus 34:29–31)

Closing prayer: Gracious God, thank you for the gift of my skin. May my skin glow radiantly in recognition of the glory of your creation.

Meditation 4

Made for Motion: Our Feet and Legs

Opening prayer: Blessed are you, God of the universe, for setting me on feet and legs. Lead me in the path of truth and service.

Wondrous Facts

A single stride requires the coordinated action of nearly two hundred muscles anchored and attached to the three large bones of the legs—the femur, the tibia, and the fibula. Our feet and legs support and propel the body.

The muscles and joints of our lower extremities provide strength and stability, flexibility and agility to the whole body. These muscles and joints also cushion and protect our bones by absorbing the shock of bone hitting bone and the friction of twisting and turning. The muscles and joints of our legs shift the weight of our body from side to side as we walk.

The toughness of our leg muscles, joints, and bones becomes clearer when we consider that during one footfall while jogging, the heel lands first, bearing the full weight of the body. The force exerted against the foot's point of contact as the heel strikes the ground, and again as the toe pushes off, is actually greater than the weight of the body.

How does the foot absorb such shock? The bones and ligaments in our foot actually loosen up in anticipation of the shock. In this loosened state, the small tarsal bones allow the foot to splay out at the sides so that these bones may nestle down into the fleshy part of the foot. This loosening happens in about one-third the time it takes to blink.

After the weight has been transferred to the front of the foot, the bones in the heel and mid-foot prepare for the second stage of a step. These bones snap together in the tightest possible formation to provide a rodlike lever to push the runner forward—all within the blinking of an eye.

Another amazing part of our leg is the knee joint, the largest, most complex joint in the body and an effective shock absorber. Unlike simple hinge joints that provide for flexing and extending, the knee joint must also provide for rotating and twisting.

Elastic tissue, called cartilage, at the ends of the bones prevents the friction of one bone rubbing against another. A large fluid-filled sac under each kneecap, called the bursa, also aids in friction protection. A smaller bursa covers the front of the knee to protect against blows and pressure.

Why doesn't all of our blood end up in our legs? After all, at any one time, the veins in our legs could hold up to fifty percent of our circulating blood. But the Creator provided two major mechanisms to keep the blood pumping to the heart. First, the leg veins are equipped with a series of valves that keep the blood flowing to the heart and do not allow reverse flow. Second, our leg muscles perform as pumps, compressing the blood vessels and forcing blood upward.

Even so, sometimes people faint after standing rigidly at attention for too long. Some slight muscle action in the legs is needed to push blood up to the heart.

Not to be forgotten is the heaviest muscle in our lower body, the gluteus maximus, or buttock muscle. This highly developed muscle provides hip extension and allows us to stand erect. One reason other primates do not spend more time standing straight is that they have proportionately smaller glutei maximi.

Reflection

Perhaps we can appreciate our feet and legs more easily than we can some other parts of our body, because they enable us to do so many things—hiking in the mountains next to clear, cold streams; climbing ladders to paint the living room; pacing back and forth while soothing a crying child; or running to our car in a rainstorm.

On the other hand, maybe we take our legs and feet for granted until something goes wrong, like breaking a bone in our foot. Perhaps the shoes we bought because they looked great, provide no support and are too flimsy. Or we may run without first warming up and pull muscles or develop shinsplints. How many of us have bum knees from athletic injuries?

God created us with feet and legs so that we could get up and around, work and play, and serve humankind. As you continue to meditate about the gift of feet and legs, keep an open spirit. Allow God to call you to a new celebration and further service.

🦶 Walk around your house barefoot for a while. Scrunch your toes into the carpet, and slide your feet over tile or wood. How does it feel? How can you use your feet to be in touch with the delightful variety of textures?

Now go for a walk outside. If the weather is just right, walk barefoot. Notice the varying textures of grass and sidewalk, sand and mud. Pay close attention to the feel of your legs and feet. Feel the muscles pulling, your knees and joints bending. As each foot hits the ground, say "thanks." Jump up and down a couple of times. If you have some music or can accompany yourself in song, do a spontaneous dance. Remember that David danced in joy before God. In offering your dance to God, celebrate the Creator by celebrating the creation of your feet and legs.

✿ Run your hands over your legs. Knead the muscles. Roll your kneecap around. Feel the muscles in your leg both tensed and relaxed. Swivel your ankle. Wonder at the intricate design and perfect utility of your legs and feet.

✿ A foot massage can relax the whole body. Ancient Asian medical practice extolls foot massage as being good for all the organs of the body. This practice, called reflexology, teaches that by massaging certain areas on the bottom of the feet, the various organs of the body also receive benefit. Foot massage may thus be healthy for the internal organs; at the very least, it always feels relaxing and can reduce the unhealthy stresses that distract us from remembering the good God who loves us.

Some people like to bathe their feet in warm water before the actual massage. You might add epsom salts or a nice-smelling bath oil or soap. As your feet soak, relax the rest of your body by tensing your muscles and then letting the tension go. Breathe deeply and slowly, in and out. Close your eyes. If you want, play some soft, soothing music, too. As you breathe, invoke the sacred name of Jesus. Pray his name as you breathe in and out.

When your foot bath is done, dry your feet by caressing them in a soft, warm towel. Take your time. Keep praying the name of Jesus.

Now massage your feet. With your fingers and thumb, knead the bottom of each foot, beginning with the heel and massaging gradually up to and including each toe. Some people use a lotion or massage oil so their hands slide easily, but mainly you want to rub your feet so that they relax.

When you have finished massaging your feet, you may want to bathe them again. Dry them carefully. And, lastly, close your eyes, breathe deeply, and plant both feet firmly on the floor. Focus your attention on your feet. Ask God to plant your feet on the way of truth and to give them good health so that you can be about the work of justice and charity.

If you have a willing friend, you might share foot massages with this person. Also, some stores that sell supplies for massage therapy carry specific devices for foot massage. Usually these devices are rolled under your foot and have ridges that knead the soles of your feet. These can be pleasant and helpful for doing foot massage.

✺ Examine your shoes. Ask yourself: "Are they good for my feet? Are they supportive, comfortable, roomy enough? Are these shoes just for looks, or do I wear them because they care for my feet?"

✺ Think of all the ways in which you used your feet and legs today to serve other people. List these ways. Then compose and pray a litany of thanks for your feet and legs as means of service—for instance, "For being able to carry in the groceries, thank you, God."

✺ Ponder meditatively the passages in "God's Word." Pick one line that strikes you as important. Pray the line over and over again, letting its meaning soak into your soul.

God's Word

Beloved: His legs are alabaster columns
set in sockets of pure gold.
His appearance is that of Lebanon,
unrivalled as the cedars.

Lover: How beautiful are your feet in their sandals,
O prince's daughter!
The curve of your thighs is like the curve of a
necklace,
work of a master hand.

(Song of Songs 5:15; 7:2)

[Jesus] poured water into a basin and began to wash the disciples' feet and to wipe them with the towel he was wearing. . . .
When he had washed their feet and put on his outer garments again he went back to the table. "Do you understand," he said, "what I have done to you? . . . If I, then, the Lord and Master, have washed your feet, you must wash each other's feet. I have given you an example so that you may copy what I have done to you." (John 13:5,12–15)

Closing prayer: As I walk this day, I thank you, gracious God, for my feet and legs. May they carry me on the way of truth, justice, and service.

Meditation 5

Deliberate Extensions: Our Arms and Hands

Opening prayer: I come to you this day, gracious God, with open arms and willing hands. May I value the gift of my arms and hands.

Wondrous Facts

Reaching out with our arms and hands must be an intentional act on our part because the muscles of our upper extremities are of the voluntary kind. This suggests that our arms and hands are extensions of ourself in a way that other body parts cannot be.

The upper extremities position the hand to work properly. Positioning the hand and fingers requires the proper and harmonious functioning of eighteen shoulder muscles, three major muscles in the upper arm, seventeen muscles in the forearm, and eighteen muscles in the hand.

Unlike the paws or claws of most other animals, the human hand works on the principle of opposability. This means that the thumb can be drawn across the palm of the hand to touch tip to tip with the other fingers—forming a grasp. That's why we can tie our shoes, write with a pen, give the Scout salute, pick up crumbs from a table, or hold the fingers of a tiny baby.

One significant and marvelous variance in human beings is hand dominance, with roughly one person in ten being left-handed. However, one-fourth of NASA's Apollo Program astronauts were left-handed, and a disproportionate number of artists, like Leonardo da Vinci and Michelangelo, show dominance in the left hand. Many geniuses, like Benjamin Franklin, are lefties. On the other hand, nearly two-thirds of autistic persons also favor their left hand. What are the connections between art, genius, autism, and left-handedness? No one seems sure. But which hand we favor seems mysteriously related to our total personality.

The palms of our hands, and especially the fingertips, are among the most sensitive parts of our body. The many different nerve endings in our skin react to an equally numerous variety of stimuli; we can thank our Meissner's corpuscles for feeling pleasant sensations from a stroke or gentle touch, for example.

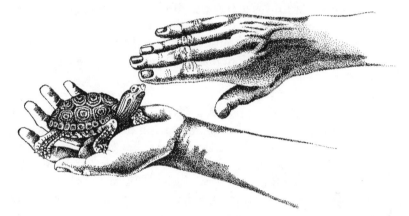

Fingernails are actually hardened skin, evolutionary remnants of the claws of our ancestors. This collection of dead skin cells, formed largely by a protein called keratin, starts at the root and takes 150 days to push out a full-length nail, growing at about one twenty-fifth of an inch per week. Our fingernails provide protective shields for the sensitive fingertips and have taken on cultural significance as places of decoration.

The shoulder joints have the widest range of joint motion in our whole body. A shallow socket for this ball-and-socket joint sacrifices stability for movement, thus making it the most easily dislocated joint in our body.

Reflection

What wonders are our arms and hands! With them we work, express our love, play music, draw, sculpt, write. Maybe our arms and hands are not easily forgotten because we use them so often. Even so, anyone who has suffered a broken arm or sprained wrist experiences an increased appreciation of the creation of hands and arms.

Praise and thanks are due God for these wonders of efficiency and function.

✍ To begin your reflections, wash your hands carefully. During this ritual act, pray these words: "I come to you, my God, with clean hands and a willing heart."

✍ Flex your hands and arms. Carefully examine the movement of the muscles and joints as you do so. Then close your eyes and, beginning with your fingers and continuing up to your shoulders, flex each muscle and bend each joint. Focus your attention on the stretching of ligaments and muscles and the bending of the joints. As you tune in to each action, pray, "Blessed be you, Creator of this wonder."

✍ Nerve endings fill our hands. As is the case with our feet, traditional Asian belief holds that by massaging the hands, the whole body benefits because of the reduction of stress. So as you did with your feet, slowly knead and massage your hands, especially the palms, but even the fingers and between the fingers. As you are doing so, breathe deeply. Pray Jesus' name, and offer God this action as an act of praise.

✍ Hugging can be a wonderful use of our arms and hands. Many people suffer from "touch deprivation," and some people fear hugs. Babies need to be touched and held; sometimes they die without such stimulation. Adults need hugs too, but are socialized out of asking for them. Consider your arms and hands as potential hugs, which can be given in all sorts of ways.
+ Who have you given a "friendly hug" to recently? This is usually a full embrace. Who, besides you, could use one?
+ A "consoling hug" may involve just resting your arm on someone's shoulder. Is there someone who needs a consoling hug?
+ A "security hug" is generally given to children, but sometimes adults need one too. This hug mostly comes in the form of a full, restful embrace. Should you give a "security hug" to anyone today?

- The "healing hug" can be cupping a broken or ill person's head in one's hands, or it can be any of the other forms of hugs, including a pat on the back. But the healing hug can also be a form of reconciliation. Do you need to give a "healing hug" to someone?
- The "celebratory hug" may include expressions like a warm embrace, holding hands, a pat on the back, or dancing. How about this? Do you want to celebrate with this kind of hug?

🜚 Prepare yourself for this guided meditation by sitting comfortably, breathing deeply, and relaxing your muscles. Close your eyes and bring to mind the presence of God. Then continue with this meditation.

You are resting in a rocking chair, rocking gently back and forth. . . . The sun shines in a window, warming your face. . . . The doorbell rings. . . . You stand and go to open it. . . . There in the doorway stands Jesus. You take a moment just to look at him. Then he reaches out his hands and arms to embrace you. . . . You extend your arms and are enfolded in his embrace. . . .

You invite Jesus into your living room and ask him to take the rocking chair. . . . You sit on a stool at his feet. . . . He asks you to tell him about your brokenness and hurts, the things that need healing. . . . You feel free to talk about anything, so you open up and share the wounded part of you. . . . As you talk, Jesus puts his hand on your shoulder. . . . He listens and every once in a while squeezes your shoulder gently. . . .

When you finish talking, Jesus puts both of his hands on your head and says, "My beloved friend, I want you to be healed and reconciled with your brothers and sisters. Have peace in your heart. May your hurts heal. I'll always be with you. Remember, I love you without reserve."

Then Jesus stands and takes your hand in his own. . . . You thank him for coming and lead him to the door. . . . Just before he departs, Jesus embraces you again. . . .

You might wish to write down some of your reactions to this encounter with Jesus. How important was his touch?

🜚 In the Scriptures, words such as *power* are associated with our hands and arms. Indeed, the act of anointing—passing on one's power—is done by the laying on of hands, usually on the kneeling person's head. Another image of hands often used in the Scriptures is that of the potter forming clay into a vessel. Meditate on the role of your hands and arms in demonstrating your abilities, your power. How do you use the power of your hands? To empower other people? Only for economic benefit? To control or manipulate other people? To make the world a little better? Are you using your hands and arms to their full potential for the good of humankind and yourself?

❧ How have you used your hands and arms for service to others during the last day or two? In your reflections, do not leave out even the smallest act of service, whether it was cleaning the toilet or carrying in the groceries. Thank the Creator for each opportunity to serve.

❧ One posture for prayer used from the earliest times is to praise God with arms and hands outstretched. As you end this time of reflection, stretch your arms and hands to heaven and give praise to God for the many ways in which your hands and arms are wonders of God's creation.

God's Word

[The truly capable woman] holds out her hands to the poor,
she opens her arms to the needy.

(Proverbs 31:20)

People were bringing little children to [Jesus], for him to touch them. . . . He embraced them, laid his hands on them and gave them his blessing. (Mark 10:13,16)

[Jesus] took the blind man by the hand and led him outside the village. Then, putting spittle on his eyes and laying his hands on him, he asked, "Can you see anything?" The man, who was beginning to see, replied, "I can see people; they look like trees as they walk around." Then he laid his hands on the man's eyes again and he saw clearly. . . . (Mark 8:23–25)

Closing prayer: Thank you, Blessed One, for the gift of my arms and hands. May I be an extension of your healing touch and loving service.

Meditation 6

Tough and Tender: Our Torso

Opening prayer: You are present here, God of love. May I rest securely in your presence, like a child resting on its parent's chest.

Wondrous Facts

The torso of the human body consists of the chest and abdomen, both of which provide protection to the vital organs that lie behind them, but are flexible when necessary. The skeletal structure of the thoracic cage—the twelve pairs of ribs and their connective tissues, the thoracic vertebrae, and the sternum (or "breastbone")—protects the heart and lungs, while also allowing the movement necessary for respiration. During one deep breath, the rib cage enlarges in three ways: the ribs swing upward and outward, the sternum pushes forward, and the diaphragm—the muscular tissue separating the contents of the chest cavity from the abdomen—descends and flattens. All this movement efficiently enlarges the cavity, making room for lung expansion.

Seven major muscle groups participate in respiration, but sometimes respiration is aided by the large muscles that normally facilitate upper-arm movement. For instance, during the explosive act of a sneeze, the large muscle in the back (known as the latissimus dorsi) contracts sharply and squeezes the rib cage.

The mammary glands lie in front of the large chest muscles called the pectoral muscles. Mammary glands are actually modified sweat glands, composed of a mesh of twenty compound glands arranged like grapes on a stalk. The size and contour of the breasts depend on the fat in the mesh of the connective tissue. During puberty, estrogen and progesterone, the two major female sexual hormones, stimulate development of the breasts and their potential for lactation (the production of milk during and after pregnancy).

During pregnancy, increased estrogen secreted by the placenta begins activation of the mammary glands, but the glands are usually prevented from releasing milk until after the baby is born. With the expulsion of the placenta and the resulting increase in prolactin (a pituitary hormone that induces lactation), milk production begins in one to three days. Increased levels of prolactin may cause each breast to swell by nearly half a pound in a single day; by the end of pregnancy, and resulting in part from the increased blood supply to the mammary glands, each breast may gain nearly one pound in weight.

Four pairs of muscles act as a corset to hold in the abdominal contents. However, the muscular wall of the abdomen allows for a great variation in the size of the cavity it protects. During pregnancy, the abdominal muscles expand greatly yet provide constant support throughout the nine months.

Reflection

Our chest and abdomen serve us as sources of protection and power, and as centers for nourishment and love. Watch a mother nurse her baby, or visualize the way a child rests its head securely on its father's chest.

However, these marvels of creation can also be sources of anxiety and lost self-esteem if we pay too much attention to the arbitrary standards set by fashion and advertising. During some periods of fashion, large breasts are "in." At other times, voluptuousness in women is "out." Advertisements for low-calorie beer make fun of chubby abdomens in men almost all the time. In other words, our chest and abdomen can become subjects of judgment about ourself.

As you meditate further, you may reappraise old attitudes about your chest and abdomen. If you have not always valued these parts of your body, take some time to do so. If you do appreciate your chest and abdomen, here are some ways of reinforcing your appreciation.

🐚 Look at your bare chest and abdomen in a mirror. What do you feel about these parts of you? If you find yourself making any judgments as to the goodness or badness of your chest or abdomen, ask yourself these questions: "On what criteria am I making these judgments? Do I agree with these standards? Would God use these criteria when looking at my chest and abdomen?" Write down your reflections.

🐚 Write a description or draw a picture of what magazines and advertisements tell you are the "ideal" breasts, or chest, and abdomen. Then write a description or draw a picture of the ways you see your own breasts, or chest, and abdomen. Does the "ideal" match your reality? If not, should you accept advertisers' standards? Would you be any healthier if you did?

🐚 Think about your body language. One very common action signifying a protective stance is crossing one's arms in front of the chest. This action is called a "barrier-signal" because it shields the chest. Do you often use this barrier-signal? Or do you move through life open and "fronting" reality?

🐚 Breast-feeding is a wonderful image of nurturing.
* *For women who have breast-fed:* Close your eyes. Relax. Recall experiences of breast-feeding your child. Surely it did not always

seem a miracle, but ponder the experience anew. What did it mean to you and to your relationship with your child? What does it mean now? Try to get in touch with the life-giving experience of breast-feeding.

* *For women who have had children but did not breast-feed:* Close your eyes. Relax. Recall the experience of holding your child at your breast. How did you feel? Was holding your child at your breast satisfying?
* *For men and women who have not had children:* When you see women breast-feeding, what are your reactions? Have you held a baby close to your chest? Have you ever bottle-fed a baby? How did you feel?

🙿 Do a thorough breast examination. As part of the care of your body, a breast examination can be very important. [Men should do this too, although breast cancer is rare among men.] First do the examination standing up. With your fingers partially spread, press lightly against your breast. Using a tight, circular massaging motion and starting at the top of each breast and moving down, feel the breast tissue. The tissue is complex, due to the arrangement of ducts, muscles, and connective tissues. Feel for any irregularities or lumps. If you do feel an irregularity in one breast, touch the other breast in the same spot for comparison.

Lie down. Repeat the examination in this position. If you find any irregularities, consult a health professional.

Do you regularly do a breast examination? If not, why not? Spend some time reflecting on this question.

Finally, ponder your reactions to this breast examination. Discuss it prayerfully with God.

🙿 Massage your abdomen in a circular hand motion. Try to breathe deeply and slowly while you are doing this. Our abdomen can hold a lot of tension. While massaging, praise God for your abdomen and for your entire body.

God's Word

Lover: How beautiful you are, how charming,
my love, my delight!
In stature like the palm tree,
its fruit-clusters your breasts. . . .
May your breasts be clusters of grapes,
your breath sweet-scented as apples,
and your palate like sweet wine.

(Song of Songs 7:7–10)

The disciple Jesus loved was reclining next to Jesus; . . . leaning back close to Jesus' chest. . . . (John 13:23–25)

Closing prayer: Blessed are you, God of life. You created my chest, breasts, and abdomen to be part of the miracle that is my body. May they be sources of care and strength.

Meditation 7

Under the Fig Leaf:
The Male Sexual Organs

Opening prayer: God of glory, I come before your presence. Increase my appreciation of male sexuality and men's sexual organs.

Wondrous Facts

Unlike women's sexual organs, which are primarily internal, men's sexual organs are located on the exterior.

The penis consists of the urethra, highly sensitive nerves, fibrous tissue, spongy tissue, arteries, and veins. The size of penises varies greatly, especially when they are flaccid. The average length of the penis when erect is about six inches, and 90 percent of men have erect penises between five and seven inches in length. During sexual stimulation, more blood enters the penis than leaves, swelling the spongy tissue and causing an erection. Teenaged males may hold an erection for up to one hour, but this time decreases to about seven minutes in old age.

The testicles hang suspended in the scrotum. The testicles consist of six hundred tightly wrapped tubes so slender that if unwrapped and stretched out, they would be several hundred feet in length. Through the action of testosterone, the male sex hormone, the testes produce about two hundred million sperm cells daily—about two hundred thousand per minute, or three thousand per second. Sperm cells mature in approximately forty-six days, and if they are not expelled, they are absorbed back into the body in a few weeks. Each sperm cell is less than five one-hundredths of an inch long and is invisible to the naked eye. In an average ejaculation, between two million and four hundred million sperm cells in about 3.5 milliliters of semen (a whitish, sticky fluid) are expelled in the course of three or four bursts, which occur about four-fifths of a second apart from each other.

Sperm containing the male sex chromosome (or Y chromosome) swim faster than those containing the female sex chromosome (or X chromosome), so the "male" sperm have a better chance of reaching the egg first. Consequently, for every 100 girls conceived, there are 125 boys conceived. Sperm cells containing the female sex chromosome are slower because they carry a heavier load of genetic material.

During sexual arousal, the penis erects, the scrotum thickens, the testes rise, the heart rate quickens, the tip of the penis swells, and the skin flushes. At ejaculation, the heart rate may climb to 130 beats per minute (nearly double the normal rate), breathing races, and blood pressure shoots up, often doubling. On average, orgasm for men lasts ten seconds.

Testosterone is the primary male sex hormone, but the testes also produce some estrogen, the female sex hormone. Levels of testosterone—and of male sexual response—reach their highest levels during the months of optimum sunlight. Levels hit bottom in winter. The highest daily levels of testosterone are produced right after sunrise.

Reflection

God gave men and women the gifts of sexual organs and sexuality. Sexuality urges us both physically and psychologically to seek completion. The biological purpose of sexual union suggests the total purpose of sexuality, that of life-giving union and fulfillment with other persons and with God.

Men are variously told to glorify their sexual organs or to denigrate them. But God created men's sexual organs as part of the male body. God's creation is good. Men's sexual organs should be valued as God's gift to men, but not as gods in themselves.

🙢 After quieting your mind by relaxing and breathing slowly, meditate on these questions:

* When I was a child, what did people say about male sexual organs?
* What attitudes did the significant adults in my life transmit to me about the penis and testicles and their functions?
* What specific incidents come to mind when I think of how my attitudes were formed?
* When I was a child, did I feel ashamed of being naked?

After spending time meditating on these questions, try to summarize the history of your attitudes about male genitals. Then ponder this question:

* How do I feel about these parts of the male body now?

🙢 Read the "Wondrous Facts" section again slowly. Ponder the function of men's sexual organs. Try to see each organ in your imagination. Praise God for each wonder.

🙢 Say these words over and over for a couple of minutes: *penis, testicles, scrotum*. How did you feel saying this? Examine the sources of these feelings.

🙢 Our sexual organs help identify us as male or female. Consequently, accepting our sexual organs as part of ourself aids in filling out our identity. Dialog with God about how well you accept and value your sexual self.

🕸 God created sexual organs to give pleasure along with the potential to reproduce. Pleasure draws humans to seek sexual union. Many men and women have been taught to be suspicious of sexual pleasure, but without the aspect of pleasure, human beings would not have a drive toward one another. In this sense, our very survival as a group depends on sexual attraction. Talk with the Creator about your experience of and attitudes about sexual pleasure.

🕸 Pray for a healing of any memories of abuse or misuse of your sexuality. Dialog with the Creator about any issues regarding your sexuality that cause you pain, anxiety, or shame.

🕸 *For men:* Do a testicular exam. Gently feel each testicle. Note any hard lumps or extremely sensitive spots on your testicles. Perform this examination periodically. Consult a physician if you detect any abnormalities.

🕸 *For men:* Stand naked in front of a mirror. Pray these affirmations:
+ For making me a man, I thank you, God.
+ For the wonder of my penis, I thank you, God.
+ For my testicles, producing the seeds for new life, I thank you, God.
+ For testosterone, I thank you, God.
+ For the sexual organs that help define me as a man, I thank you, God.
+ For the great gift of sexuality, I thank you, God.

🕸 Meditate on "God's Word" and discuss these questions with God in prayer:
+ Am I ashamed of my sexuality or my sexual organs because I do not accept them as, in some way, made in God's own image?
+ If so, how can I begin to feel better about this gift?

God's Word

In Eden, Adam and Eve were naked, the man and the woman, "but they felt no shame before each other" (Genesis 2:25). When they fell into the sin of disbelieving that they were made in God's image, they became ashamed of their nakedness: "Then the eyes of both of them were opened and they realised that they were naked. So they sewed fig-leaves together to make themselves loin-cloths" (Genesis 3:7).

Closing prayer: Thank you, God, for the beauty of male sexuality, for the parts of the male body that give pleasure and call forth from men the desire for unity and love.

Meditation 8

Form Follows Function: The Female Sexual Organs

Opening prayer: God of glory, I come before your presence. Increase my appreciation of women's sexual organs and the great gift of female sexuality.

Wondrous Facts

Unlike men, women have both external and internal sexual organs.

Women's internal sexual organs include two ovaries, about the size of walnuts; two Fallopian tubes, each about four inches long, that connect the ovaries to the uterus; the uterus, a pear-shaped, hollow, muscular organ a bit smaller than a woman's fist; and the four- to five-inch-long vagina, or birth canal.

The external organs include the vulva; pairs of labia, outer and inner lips that conceal the opening to the vagina; the urethra, which leads from the bladder; and, located above the entrance to the vagina, the clitoris—an organ very responsive to sexual stimulation. The clitoris contains erectile tissue, like that of the penis, that fills with blood during sexual stimulation. The length of the clitoris varies greatly, but around a quarter of an inch is average.

Women's sexual maturity begins with menstruation, the onset of which is two or three years earlier than it was a century ago, probably due to diet. Menopause, or the cessation of menstruation and fertility, usually occurs between the ages of thirty-five and fifty-five, with the average age being forty-nine. However, even though menopause ends fertility, many women find their sexual responsiveness increasing at mid-life.

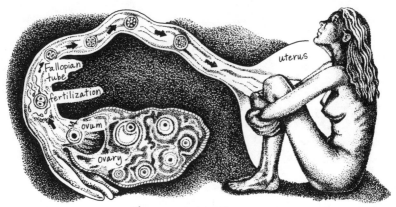

The movement to life

At birth, a female child's ovaries contain between forty thousand and three hundred thousand egg cells. When a girl reaches puberty, these eggs begin to emerge at an average of one every twenty-eight days, with the release of the egg alternating by month between the two ovaries. The ovaries release approximately four hundred eggs during an average thirty-five-year period of fertility.

This finite childbearing span can be somewhat offset by multiple births. A Soviet woman gave birth to sixty-nine children in twenty-seven pregnancies. She bore sixteen pairs of twins, seven sets of triplets, and four sets of quadruplets. Today's most prolific mothers are Kenyans, who bear an average of eight children per woman. The world average is four children per woman.

Sexual response in women follows a similar pattern to that found in men, with increasing heart rate and rising blood pressure, flushed skin and dilated pupils. During sexual stimulation, the vagina lubricates and the clitoris lengthens. The nipples become erect and sensitive. The outer labia open and flatten, while the inner labia swell and extend outward. The uterus moves up and away from the vagina. In the climactic phase, the outer part of the vagina contracts, the outer labia swell further, and the inner labia turn dark red. At orgasm, the vagina contracts strongly every four-fifths of a second, from three to as many as twelve times. Unlike men, women can experience multiple orgasms, several within a few minutes.

When intercourse takes place during a woman's fertile period, it takes from six to thirty-six hours for a sperm to penetrate the egg. After fertilization occurs, the average pregnancy lasts 266 days. All during pregnancy, the muscular uterus improves its muscle tone by squeezing for twenty-second bursts every twenty minutes. These involuntary contractions prepare the uterus for the contractions of birth, which will enlarge the cervix from the size of a large dot (around the size of the *o* in *dot*) to approximately four inches in diameter. The uterus weighs about three pounds after nine months of pregnancy and has, temporarily, the strongest muscles in a woman's body. This can be attested to by obstetricians who, while putting their fingers into the cervix during childbirth, have suffered broken fingers as a result of uterine contractions.

Reflection

God gave women and men the gifts of sexual organs and sexuality. Sexuality urges us both physically and psychologically to seek completion. The biological purpose of sexual union suggests the total purpose of sexuality, that of life-giving union and fulfillment with other persons and with God.

Despite these wonders of creation—women's sexual organs—many women have been taught to be ashamed of their sexuality. Manufacturers aim a whole range of products toward covering up or sanitizing the natural functions of women's bodies. Sometimes women receive the implication that their bodies are valuable only insofar as they bear children. Certainly this act of co-creation is a wonderful gift, but women's bodies are part of what makes women full human beings, whether they bear children or not.

After quieting your mind by relaxing and breathing slowly, meditate on these questions:
+ When I was a child, what did people say about female sexual organs?
+ What attitudes did the significant adults in my life transmit to me about the vagina, ovaries, uterus, clitoris, and their functions?
+ What specific incidents come to mind when I think of how my attitudes were formed?
+ When I was a child, did I feel ashamed of being naked?

After spending time meditating on these questions, try to summarize the history of your attitudes about female genitals. Then ponder this question:

• How do I feel about these parts of the female body now?

🕮 Read the "Wondrous Facts" section again slowly. Ponder the function of each of women's sexual organs. Try to see each organ in your imagination. Praise God for each wonder.

🕮 Say these words over and over for a couple of minutes: *vagina, ovaries, uterus, clitoris*. How did you feel saying this? Examine the sources of these feelings.

🕮 Our sexual organs help identify us as male or female. Consequently, accepting our sexual organs as part of ourself aids in filling out our identity. Dialog with God about how well you accept and value your sexual self.

🕮 God created sexual organs to give pleasure along with the potential to reproduce. Pleasure draws humans to seek sexual union. Many women and men have been taught to be suspicious of sexual pleasure, but without the aspect of pleasure, human beings would not have a drive toward one another. In this sense, our very survival as a group depends on sexual attraction. Talk with the Creator about your experience of and attitudes about sexual pleasure.

🕮 From biblical times, menstruation came to be considered a curse. Judaic law called menstruating women "unclean" and required their "purification." On a physical level, menstruation for some women can be accompanied by discomfort, mood swings, and pain. Meditate for a while on your own attitudes about menstruation. Ponder the essential value of menstruation and what it means in the full cycle of a woman's life. How can it be considered a wonderful gift? Talk to the Creator about this aspect of female sexuality.

🕮 Share with Jesus, the Healer, any memories of abuse or misuse of your sexuality, and any issues regarding your sexuality that cause you pain, anxiety, or shame. Talk directly to Jesus, the Healer, remembering his compassion to suffering and scarred people.

✿ Meditate on "God's Word" and discuss these questions with God in prayer:

* Am I ashamed of my sexuality or my sexual organs because I do not accept them as, in some way, made in God's own image?
* If so, how can I begin to feel better about this gift?

✿ *For women:* Stand naked in front of a mirror. Pray these affirmations:

* For making me a woman, I thank you, God.
* For the wonder of my ovaries, capable of giving new life, I thank you, God.
* For the amazing Fallopian tubes, which carry forth the eggs, I thank you, God.
* For the uterus, cradle of potential life, I thank you, God.
* For the clitoris, source of the gift of sexual pleasure, I thank you, God of life.
* For my vagina and all the parts of me that make me sexually a woman, I thank you, God.

God's Word

In Eden, Adam and Eve were naked, the man and the woman, "but they felt no shame before each other" (Genesis 2:25). When they fell into the sin of disbelieving that they were made in God's image, they became ashamed of their nakedness: "Then the eyes of both of them were opened and they realised that they were naked. So they sewed fig-leaves together to make themselves loin-cloths" (Genesis 3:7).

Closing prayer: Thank you, God, for all the marvels of women's sexuality. I praise your infinite wisdom and ask your blessings as I try to cherish and nurture the fullness of this gift.

Meditation 9

Working Partners:
Our Bones and Muscles

Opening prayer: God of power and might, may I grow in strength and courage so as to use my bones and muscles for the good of your people and all of creation.

Wondrous Facts

Our bones act as an internal scaffolding, providing a framework for the body's soft structures. Newborns have around 350 individual bones, but as children grow, their bones fuse. The newborn's loosely connected bones allow the skull to change shape right before birth so that the head will fit the narrow confines of the birth canal. Thereafter, the conical shape of the head quickly changes back to the normal shape of the skull.

By adulthood, we have a skeleton composed of 206 bones. However, some of us have a few extra bones, possibly an extra rib or vertebra.

The strength of our human scaffolding is incredible. Bone can withstand a stress of twenty-four thousand pounds per square inch, or about four times the stress capability of steel or reinforced concrete. This strength becomes more amazing when we consider that 25 percent of bone is water, 30 percent is living tissue—cells and blood vessels—and 45 percent consists of mineral deposits like calcium phosphate. And bone tissue is constantly being destroyed and replaced. About every seven years, the body grows the equivalent of an entirely new skeleton.

Have you ever wondered about the differences between female and male skeletons? The work of anthropologists who study grave sites provides us with these key distinctions: Females have wider and shorter breastbones, slimmer wrists, and smaller, smoother jaws and skulls. The male skull has a more slanted forehead and heavier brow ridges. Even though the male skeleton is usually larger, females have a wider pelvis with a large round birth opening in the center. The male pelvic opening is smaller and shaped somewhat like a heart.

Bones provide our scaffolding, but they also perform other essential roles. Bone marrow, the tissue at the center of the long bones and sternum, produces red blood cells, white blood cells, and platelets—all of which are necessary for life. The outsides of bones release calcium, which is essential for nerve impulse transmissions, muscle contractions, and blood clotting.

Surrounding our bones (and sometimes being surrounded by our bones) are over 650 muscles of three basic types: voluntary muscle, involuntary muscle, and cardiac muscle. Voluntary muscles, attached to the skeleton by tendons, aid the body in conscious movement. Involuntary muscles line our internal organs and contract automatically to regulate the functioning of the stomach and intestines, blood vessels, glands, and so on. Cardiac muscle, which controls the heart, has many characteristics of both voluntary and involuntary muscle.

Imagine that you are typing. When you move your fingers over the keyboard, your body is already sending nerve impulses from the brain along outgoing, or "motor," nerve pathways to the appropriate muscles in your arms. Although these nerve impulses act like an electric current passing along a fine wire, they are in fact a ripple of chemical activity surging along the nerve membrane to a contact point at the muscle. At this contact point, signal chemicals are released that transmit the impulse from the nerve ending to the muscle fiber. These chemicals trigger an interaction between two major chemicals in the muscles, which causes the muscle fibers to shorten, or contract. (Muscles always work by contracting or pulling, never by pushing—not even in push-ups.)

Muscles also work in pairs, so that when a muscle on one side of our arm contracts to lift something, the muscle on the other side relaxes. When we put down the object, the muscle that was relaxed contracts, and its opposite relaxes. Clearly, if we had to give conscious directions to initiate each step in the process, typing a letter might take years.

To understand the power of our muscles, consider this: when our body experiences severe cold, shivering produces heat and warms us by forcing the muscles to contract and relax rapidly—a bit like vigorously rubbing two sticks together to make fire. About 80 percent of the muscle energy generated turns into heat—enough, at times, to boil a quart of water for one hour.

Our longest muscle, the sartorius, extends from the waist to the knee and flexes both the hip and the knee. The strongest muscle is the gluteus maximus (the rump muscle), which moves the thighbone (or femur). The largest muscle is the latissimus dorsi, the flat muscle of the back that allows arm rotation. One of the tiniest muscles (one-twentieth of an inch in length), the stapedius, activates the stirrup bone in our ear that sends vibrations from the eardrum to the inner ear. The fastest muscles are those in the eye, which contract in less than one one-hundredth of a second. The happiest muscles are those not needed to frown: over twice as many muscles are used in a scowl than are used in a smile. So smile!

Reflection

Thankfully, we seldom need to think about our bones and muscles. They work away in obscurity, only complaining and stopping when they are pushed beyond their limits. Bones and muscles power our ability to serve, to love, or to act. In the Hebrew Scriptures, woman and man were "bone of [the other's] bones." To express a conviction or emotion that is profound, we say it is felt "deep in my bones." Bones and muscles give form to our dreams.

❧ Read "Wondrous Facts" again. Stop and meditate on one or two of the facts that most amaze you. Dialog with the Creator about your amazement.

❧ Stoop over slowly and pick up an object. Concentrate on feeling the various muscles contracting and stretching. Then get down on all fours on the floor. Pretend that you are a cat. Arch your back, stretching all of your large back muscles. Then roll your head around like a cat does when it starts to unwind. Next, still assuming your feline role, stretch your left leg out behind you as far as you can; hold your leg out as long as possible, and then repeat the process with your right leg. Arch your back again. Ponder all the muscles at work.

❧ Starting from your feet and going to the top of your head, run your hands over as many of your bones and muscles as you can feel. By pressing in with your fingers, try to outline each muscle and bone. Notice how muscles connect to bones at the joints. Flex each muscle and touch it. Then massage the muscle. Bend or swivel each joint. Take your time.

As you flex, swivel, touch, and massage each bone and muscle, recall how this particular bone or muscle serves you. Then thank God out loud for the muscle or bone, for example, "Thank you, Creator, for the spinal column that protects my spinal cord, helps me to stand up, and enables me to work."

❧ Recall from your body history any instances when you broke a bone, sprained a joint, or pulled a muscle. List each of these injuries. Then write a brief summary of how each injury affected you, how long your recovery took, and what activities you were restricted from because of the injury. Thank God for healing.

☙ To serve us so that we can serve other people, our bones and muscles require exercise. Without exercise, muscles weaken and bones deteriorate. Exercise tones our muscles, adds to our strength, increases our endurance, improves our circulation, and so on. Physical inactivity can result in tiredness, back pain, weight gain, a sluggish blood flow, digestive problems, and a host of other maladies.

Review your patterns of exercise and inactivity. Try to list all the physical activities you engaged in during the last week. Rate each activity from 1 (very light exercise, such as shopping or bowling) to 5 (very heavy exercise, such as running or dancing).

Then spend some time pondering and answering these questions:

* Am I getting enough exercise to keep my bones and muscles in good working order?
* If not, what practical steps can I take to develop my body for the good of myself, humankind, and God?

☙ As you work during the next twenty-four hours, pay close attention occasionally to the muscles and bones you are using. For instance, if you are sitting at a desk typing, stop for a moment with your hands poised above the keyboard and reflect on all the muscles that help you sit up in your chair, hold your arms out, and make your fingers find the right keys. Praise God for these muscles and bones. Later, when you are driving (don't stop in traffic), consider all the muscles and bones being employed. Again, praise God.

☙ Inventory all the ways in which you use your muscles and bones in the service of other people. Do an examen of consciousness to find out if you are sufficiently aware of your ability to serve others.

God's Word

A kindly glance gives joy to the heart,
  good news lends strength to the bones.

(Proverbs 15:30)

The Creator wanted to give the human being a companion with whom to share the Garden of Eden. So while the human being slept, God took a rib from the human's side with which to create a companion.

When one of the humans woke, he discovered that he was a man. Looking over, he realized that he had a companion and exclaimed, "How wonderful! This other human is bone of my bone and flesh of my flesh. She is woman!" The woman woke and smiled at the man. Both of them were naked, but they felt no shame in front of each other. (Adapted from Genesis 2:21–25)

Closing prayer: God of wonder, bless these bones and muscles of mine. May I use their strength well to build the earth and to create your Reign in our midst.

Meditation 10

The Heart of the Matter: Our Heart and Circulation

Opening prayer: Live in my heart, gracious God. Enliven me! Fill my being with faith, hope, and love, just as my heart fills my body with life-giving blood.

Wondrous Facts

Weighing only about ten ounces, the heart is not much larger than a clenched fist, yet it is a marvelous circulatory organ. Contracting at approximately seventy beats per minute, it pumps enough blood in a lifetime to fill thirteen supertankers, each holding one million barrels.

The right ventricle pumps blue, oxygen-depleted blood to the lungs in order to receive oxygen. When this blood, now oxygenated, returns to the left ventricle, the heart pumps it out to the rest of the body. During the day, nearly two thousand gallons of blood flow through the heart's chambers.

To do its work, the heart has unique electrical properties that give it the ability to continue beating even outside the body. If you ever dissected a frog in a biology class, you likely recall the throbbing heart of your victim. Cardiac muscle cells will continue to pulse until they are severely damaged by a loss of oxygen or by other physical or chemical changes to their surrounding environment. Like all muscles, the heart needs toning and strengthening from exercise and proper nutrition.

The pump of life

The circulatory system consists of sixty thousand miles of arteries, arterioles, capillaries, venules, and veins, all carrying blood throughout the body. Because of the body's constant need for oxygen, the respiratory and circulatory systems are intricately connected. A slight change in one system causes immediate changes in the other.

Our blood consists of four essential components: red blood cells, white blood cells, platelets, and the fluid plasma—in which the previous three components are suspended.

Red blood cells number about twenty-five trillion in the average adult body, throughout which they transport oxygen and pick up carbon dioxide, the waste product that is carried to the lungs for expulsion. Red blood cells circuit the body up to three hundred thousand times in their 120-day life span. Three million replacement cells are being manufactured by the bone marrow each minute.

Though fewer in number, white blood cells protect the body against disease-causing germs by producing antibodies. White blood cells actually eat and digest foreign bacteria. The lymph nodes, spleen, thymus, and bone marrow all produce white blood cells, without which we would have to live in a completely sterile environment to protect ourselves from common bacteria and viruses, the simplest of which could be life-threatening.

Finally, platelets are responsible for forming blood clots whenever bleeding occurs. In severe trauma—lacerations or punctures—clotting can begin in fifteen seconds.

Reflection

The heart has become a symbol of affection, passion, and life itself. Indeed, any kind of strong emotion causes a response in the heart. Strong feelings stir the heart to beat faster.

The heart may be a symbol of love, but many of us need to love our own heart. After all, how can we serve other people, love other people, if we do not have a healthy heart ourself? Don't just *have* a heart! Value, appreciate, and nurture the heart you have.

❦ Read "Wondrous Facts" again. Find one passage or fact that strikes you as being especially amazing. Dialog with Jesus about why this fact means so much to you.

❦ Take your pulse. Find your pulse either at your wrist or right in front of your ear. While sitting quietly, count the beats for ten seconds and then multiply this count by six to find your pulse rate. Or just feel the blood being pumped from your heart, giving life to your body. Then get up and walk around, or maybe walk up some stairs. Now take your pulse again. Notice the variation.

We can slow our heart rate by using the relaxation and meditation methods already employed in some of the earlier reflections. Sit quietly in a chair, letting your hands rest in your lap. Systematically relax your whole body, starting with your feet and going all the way up to your head. Breathe deeply and slowly, in through your nose and out through your mouth. Picture a favorite place in nature, a place you always find relaxing, and mentally situate yourself there for a while. Continue your deep breathing. After a time, take your pulse again.

Ponder the fact that your heart is always adapting to your level of activity, and that you can aid your heart through some simple relaxation techniques. Praise God for your heart.

❦ If you can find a stethoscope, listen to the beating of your heart.

❦ According to the Book of Proverbs, "Worry makes a heart heavy, / a kindly word makes it glad" (12:25). Modern medical science has added its voice to reaffirm this principle. Worry stresses the heart. Kindness is an antidote. Imagine that you are in a dialog with your heart. Write down your discussion about these questions:

* Me: What do I worry about that puts too much stress on you?
Heart: To start with . . .
[Continue discussing any worries that may be stressful and useless.]
* Me: Well, now that you've told me about all my useless worries, what can I do about them?
Heart: Think about that first worry. How about . . .
[Dialog until you have talked about coping with your worries.]
* Me: What kind words and deeds make you glad and take off some of the pressure?
Heart: You normally ignore Juan, but yesterday . . .
[Talk with your heart about how to build more kindness into your lifestyle.]

✤ If you have not checked your blood pressure for a while, go out of your way to have this done in the next day or so. When you get the results, ponder their meaning for you. If you need to bring the pressure down, seek medical advice and pray over the matter.

✤ Review your diet. Is it a heart-healthy diet? Do you eat too much salt, cholesterol, or saturated fat? Are you nourishing your body with good foods?

✤ In Matthew 6:21, Jesus says, "'Wherever your treasure is, there will your heart be too.'" Meditate on this phrase; repeat it over and over again slowly.
    Relax. Breathe deeply, evenly, and slowly. . . . Look inward, and concentrate on your breathing. . . . Slow the beating of your heart. . . . Relax your muscles by flexing them and then letting go of all tension. . . . Recall the presence of the living God once again. . . .
    Now bring to mind all the treasures where your heart is . . . start with the people-treasures of your life. See their faces. . . . Greet them and touch them in a way that cherishes them. . . .
    Now look at your other treasures. . . . Bring them to mind, one by one. . . .
    Is God one of your treasures? . . . Are any poor or sick or helpless people among your treasures? . . . Are there any material "treasures" not deserving of so much of your heart? . . .
    Praise God for the truly valuable treasures of your heart. . . .

God's Word

Hope deferred makes the heart sick,
desire fulfilled is a tree of life.

(Proverbs 13:12)

"Yahweh our God is the one, the only Yahweh. You must love Yahweh your God with all your heart, with all your soul, with all your strength. Let the words I enjoin on you today stay in your heart." (Deuteronomy 6:4–6)

Closing prayer: God of love and gladness, set my heart at rest, and guide my heart toward the true treasures of love and mercy, peace and goodwill. May I treat my heart, and the hearts of all people I meet, with compassion.

Meditation 11

The Breath of Life: Our Lungs

Opening prayer: Come, Breath of Life. Come, Spirit of God. May I praise you in every breath I take.

Wondrous Facts

The ancients believed that the winds stirring the world were magical and that air was the sovereign element of the cosmos. Science has instructed us about the composition of air, yet it still seems magical that every breath in our lungs stirs our body to life—like a kite in a gentle, steady breeze.

As we breathe, our lungs transfer oxygen to the bloodstream (and in particular, to the red blood cells) and remove the carbon dioxide waste. The respiratory and circulatory systems work jointly to accomplish this essential exchange.

The respiratory system adapts amazingly to our body's changing need for oxygen. While we sleep, each breath lasts four to six seconds and involves about one pint of air. But when we run for a bus, climb stairs, or dig in the garden, the amount of air needed may increase by as much as twenty times; during such physical exertion, both the rate of respiration and the amount of air taken in per breath are increased. A person needs about eight quarts of air per minute when lying down, sixteen quarts when sitting, twenty-four quarts when walking, and fifty or more quarts when running. In a lifetime, the average person breathes about seventy-five million gallons of air.

Our lungs are paired, spongelike organs that are constructed of lobes, or sections—three lobes in the right lung and two lobes in the left; the heart occupies the remaining space on the left side of the chest cavity. Air entering through the nose and mouth is sucked down the trachea (or "windpipe") into the deepest part of the lungs. The trachea forks into two branches, called bronchi, from which other tubes branch off—like limbs on a tree—and become progressively smaller, ending in millions of tiny air sacs through which the oxygen and carbon dioxide are exchanged. The tissue that forms these air sacs, or alveoli, is only 1/250,000 of an inch thick. The average nonsmoker has approximately three hundred million alveoli. Smoking breaks down these air sacs, greatly reducing their number and, consequently, the space for the oxygen and carbon dioxide exchange.

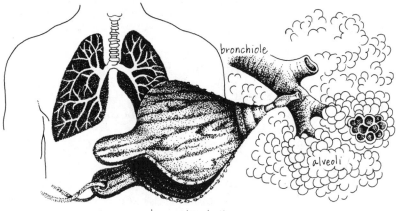

Lungs like bellows

When we breathe in, the thoracic cage enlarges—much like a bellows when the handles are pulled apart. As the chest area enlarges, the pressure within it decreases, creating a slight vacuum. This negative pressure pulls air through the upper passageways into the alveoli. The reverse happens during exhalation. Compression of the thoracic cage increases the pressure around and within the lungs, and air is forced out.

Many factors regulate respiration. Higher levels of carbon dioxide directly increase respiration, as do exercise, oxygen deprivation (for instance, at high altitudes), fright, stress, and illness. An increase of only 0.3 percent in carbon dioxide content doubles the volume of air breathed in and out.

Healthy lungs have more than enough capacity to fulfill the body's oxygen needs. With a total surface area roughly the size of a tennis court, the lungs provide sufficient space for nearly three hundred billion capillaries to interact with the alveoli. If stretched out end to end, the capillaries in the lungs would reach from New York to Florida—about one thousand miles.

To protect the upper airways and lungs from disease-carrying organisms, we have hairlike cilia that continually move mucus and other foreign particles up and out of the lungs. Smoking destroys cilia, as does breathing heavily polluted air. City dwellers breathe in roughly twenty million particles of foreign matter each day. Thus, living in a smog-permeated city can have a destructive effect on our lungs similar to smoking.

Reflection

Our lungs play a vital role in the life and health of our body, and they are equipped to protect themselves from damage. But today, with ever-increasing amounts of air pollution, our lungs are often being overwhelmed by destructive substances. Our efforts to keep the air clean take on additional meaning when we ponder this wonder of God's creation, our lungs.

Slow, deep breathing can be a source of relaxation and stress reduction. The flow of life-giving air in and out of our lungs becomes a natural prayer when we focus our attention on it and on the Maker of our lungs.

🙏 Read "Wondrous Facts" again. Find one passage or fact that strikes you as being especially amazing. Dialog with Jesus about what this fact means to you.

🙏 Find a comfortable position. Many people find that they breathe most easily while sitting in a straightbacked chair. Focus your attention on your own breathing process. Attend your breath as it flows in and out of your lungs. Breathe so deeply that your inflating lungs push out your abdomen. Try breathing in through your nose—this way the air is warmed and moistened before entering the lungs. Breathe out through your mouth. If thoughts do pop into your mind, just let them flow through; calmly refocus on your breathing.

Do this for five to ten minutes with your eyes closed, and then stand up, stretch, smile, and continue with your daily activities.

✍ God breathes life into us at every moment and is present in the life that surrounds us. Without breathing, we would die in minutes. In a comfortable breathing position, close your eyes and focus on your breathing again. Spend some minutes just relaxing, breathing slowly, rhythmically, and deeply. . . .

Then, as you breathe, ponder the fact that the air—your source of life—is filled with God's loving presence. . . . Imagine that the air you breathe is the breath of the Creator, making you anew. . . . As you inhale, you are drawing in the life of your Creator. . . .

As you breathe out, let go of all your worries, anger, and stress. . . . Breathe in the loving God, breathe out all that is unhealthy and unloving. . . . Try to picture the things that bother you leaving your lungs and being exhaled. . . .

Imagine that your whole body, starting with your lungs, is suffused with the light and Spirit of the living God. . . .

Meditate in the presence of this light. . . .

✍ Lie down on your back. Rest your hands lightly on your chest (to make sure that it does not move). Then try to breathe only into your belly. Breathe into your belly for several moments. (You might put a pillow under your knees to take the strain off of your legs and lower back.)

Now, with your hands resting gently on your chest, breathe into your chest. Notice how it swells and depresses. Breathe only into your chest for a while.

Next, breathe in and out as you normally do. Which are you, a chest breather or a belly breather? Which is more comfortable?

Practice deep breathing. This is done by filling your belly first and then letting the air expand your chest. Try this. Relax (do not lift your shoulders) and breathe deeply, filling your belly first and then filling the chest. Do this deep breathing with one hand on your belly and the other on your chest to monitor the pattern. Breathe in and out deeply, following the motion of your breath and hands. Do this until you feel calm and relaxed. This kind of deep breathing is a great way to reduce stress.

❧ In rhythm with your breathing, pray the words *Come, Spirit*, or *Jesus*, or use these names for God from the Scriptures: *Wind, Breath, Breeze*. As you pray God's name, ponder this idea: you share the air with all of life on this planet and with the universe. Air connects us with the cosmos.

❧ In order to nurture our lungs and the lungs of our sisters and brothers, the air we breathe must be clean. Pollution comes in many forms. Spend some time meditating on the air you breathe and what you might do to clean it and thereby clean your lungs.

* Is my car tuned so that it burns gas efficiently? Do I use my car more than necessary?
* Do I smoke? Do I tolerate cigarette or cigar smoke?
* Do I keep in mind, when I heat, cool, or light my home, that the amount of energy I use has an impact on the cleanliness of the air?
* Am I committed to recycling, so that less garbage will be burned?
* How else can I contribute to clean air for my lungs and the lungs of all my sisters and brothers?

Pray to the Creator for a greater commitment to clean air for all of our lungs.

God's Word

The Creator formed the first human being out of the soil and breathed the breath of life into the nose of this first human. (Adapted from Genesis 2:7)

Praise to you, Yahweh, with resounding cymbals;
praise with clanging cymbals.
Let everything that has breath praise Yahweh.
Alleluia.

(Psalm 150:5–6)

[Jesus] breathed on them and said:
Receive the Holy Spirit.

(John 20:22)

Closing prayer: Come, Holy Spirit. Breath of Life, come fill my lungs, fill my being. May my intentions be as pure in spirit as the breath in my lungs. May every breath be an act of praise to you!

Meditation 12

The Outside In:
Our Digestive System

Opening prayer: Courteous God, you invite us to dine at your table. You nourish us with food and drink. Thank you for my marvelous digestive system. May I appreciate it and treat it well.

Wondrous Facts

The logic of digestion and absorption is best understood when it is realized that a human being is a kind of fancy-shaped doughnut, whose digestive tract is the hole in the middle. Although we talk of our intestines as our "insides," food in the intestine is in fact still outside the body. The object of digestion is to reduce that food to particles small enough to pass across the "inner skin" of the intestinal wall and into the body. (Claire Rayner, ed., *Atlas of the Body*, p. 44)

From mouth to anus, our digestive tract runs about twenty-six feet. The length of our digestive tract matches that of most herbivores, suggesting that we were created primarily as plant eaters. It is this length that allows for efficient digestion and absorption of plant nutrients; carnivores, on the other hand, have short digestive systems that allow them to quickly process and eliminate large amounts of protein, fat, and cholesterol.

Digestion begins in the mouth, initiated by the tongue, where nine thousand taste buds can analyze and identify food flavors in a

tenth of a second. The taste buds are actually clusters of chemore-
ceptors, each equipped with a small hairlike projection on its upper
surface and linked below with nerve fibers. The tongue can identify
four tastes: saltiness and sweetness are sensed best by the front of the
tongue, sourness by the sides, and bitterness by the back. The
tongue's center has virtually no taste sensation, but its front two-
thirds quickly senses temperature, pain, and touch.

Taste also depends on smell. People need approximately twenty-five thousand times as much of a substance in their mouth to taste
it as they need to detect it by smell. Adults lose some of their taste
buds over time, which may explain why bland food is called
"pablum" by adults seeking a little zing from what they eat; to be
tasted, adults' food requires more flavoring.

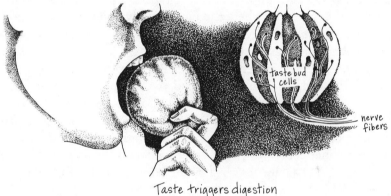

Taste triggers digestion

Taste buds start the digestive process by stimulating the production of saliva, to the measure of three or four pints per day. Like
other plant eaters, our saliva contains an enzyme that has the sole
purpose of breaking down some of the complex carbohydrates found
in plant food.

Imagine that you are eating a hamburger. The very sight, smell,
or sometimes even thought of it can stimulate the next step—the
flow of gastric juice in the stomach. Gastric juice is composed of digestive enzymes, needed for the breakdown of foods; hydrochloric
acid, which aids in chemical action and kills bacteria; and mucus,
which protects the lining of the stomach from digesting itself.

As you chew (remember, eat slowly and chew your food), saliva breaks down some of the bun's starch. The food is then pushed
down the esophagus to the stomach, a distensible sac with a holding

capacity of about two or three pints. Through the digestive and con-tractive actions of the stomach, your burger has become chyme—a watery mixture of partly digested food and digestive secretions. Your burger is definitely well-done at this point; hydrochloric acid has even melted the fat.

The stomach pushes the burger (or what used to be a burger) into the duodenum, a ten-inch section of the small intestine where digestion really gets under way. To neutralize the acid produced in the stomach, the pancreas secretes alkaline digestive juices into the small intestine. Each day, about a quart of pancreatic juice is need-ed. The liver and gallbladder contribute bile to help break up fats in the small intestine. In addition to all this activity, complex muscle contractions in the small intestine churn, knead, and segment the remains of the burger into small enough particles to pass through the wall of the intestine, where the blood and lymph vessels transport these nutrients to the liver and other organs. By this time the burg-er is doing you some nutritional good.

The last two segments of the small intestine are the jejunum, stretching eight feet in length, and the ileum, twelve feet long. These two segments complete the digestion and absorption of your erstwhile burger. Absorption within the intestines is a highly effi-cient operation. Between food, drink, and gastrointestinal secretions, the intestines cope with two to three gallons of fluid a day. Of these gallons, almost all are absorbed by the body; only one-fifth of a pint is lost in feces.

After the small intestine has done its work, your burger—by now watery chyme, fibrous waste, indigestible cellulose, some salts, and unwanted breakdown products—is pushed into the six-foot-long large intestine, or colon, where more water is absorbed and fe-ces are formed.

The net result of this digestive operation is the supremely effi-cient acquisition of energy. To realize the effectiveness of our diges-tive system, consider this: the food energy contained in three ounces of carbohydrate (equivalent to about 1.4 ounces of gasoline) is enough to fuel someone to ride a bicycle for an hour at a speed of ten miles per hour. If our bodies used gasoline instead of food, we could ride over nine hundred miles on one gallon of gas. How's that for fuel efficiency?

Reflection

"We are what we eat" is a cliché that makes some sense. We depend on the energy produced from what we eat. To continue the car analogy, if we put adulterated gas into our car, the engine will miss, backfire, or maybe die on us. Sugar in a gas tank can cause the engine to seize up, doing costly damage. Given the right care and maintenance, our digestive system will remain a marvel of efficient operation. If we can treat our car with such loving care, we can care for our digestive system just as diligently.

The Creator calls human beings to nourish themselves. Jesus reminds his followers that they have a duty to nourish all their sisters and brothers as well. Appreciating our digestion needs to be part of an appreciation for our responsibility to feed the hungry and give drink to the thirsty.

❧ Ponder your own digestive system. In your mind's eye, follow an orange (or some other favorite food) from your mouth, down the esophagus, into the stomach, to the small and then the large intestine, and out the rectum and anus. What happens to the food? You need not be a biologist to do this; just tap into your own experience of digestion.

To make this meditation more tangible, eat some crunchy vegetable or fruit. Chew slowly, savor the taste, and feel the texture. Pay attention to your swallowing. Then imagine what happens as this tasty morsel becomes energy.

To make this meditation still more concrete, draw or color this act of digestion. Try to demonstrate your perception and experience of what happens.

❧ Keep a log of your eating and drinking habits for one week. Write down what you ate, where you ate, how long each meal took, and how you felt before, during, and after eating. Are there any emotional cues that prompt you to eat more or less than you should? Are there any foods that you should leave alone or ones that you should add to your diet? At the end of each day, and also at the end of the week, summarize what you learned about your eating patterns. Talk about your eating behavior with your Creator. Are there any patterns you want to continue, or any you would like to change? Ask for the strength and wisdom to eat properly.

❧ How are you getting along with your digestive system? Engage your digestive system in an imaginary conversation. Talk to it about how you two have gotten along in the past, what habits your relationship has developed, what changes you might want to agree upon to make the relationship more healthy, what foods pose particular difficulties, and so on. This discussion just might help your relationship.

❧ As we value our own digestion, we might gain even more empathy for people who suffer the agony of hunger, people who have nothing to digest, people hovering at death's door. Meditate on your response to the hunger of other people. Is there more you can do to help feed the hungry of our world? In feeding hungry people we honor God and our own life.

❧ Read "God's Word" and pick out one phrase that strikes you as especially helpful. Pray with this phrase for a while, letting it speak to you. As a follow-up, write about what this phrase said to your mind and heart.

God's Word

The Son of man came, eating and drinking. . . . (Matthew 11:19)

[After Jesus' resurrection] he himself stood among them and said to them, "Peace be with you!" In a state of alarm and fright, they thought they were seeing a ghost. . . . "Touch me and see for yourselves; a ghost has no flesh. . . ." Their joy was so great that they still could not believe it, as they were dumbfounded; so he said to them, "Have you anything here to eat?" And they offered him a piece of grilled fish, which he took and ate before their eyes. (Luke 24:36–43)

A moderate diet ensures sound sleep,
　　one gets up early, in the best of spirits.
Sleeplessness, biliousness and gripe
　　are what the glutton has to endure.
Wine gives life
　　if drunk in moderation.

What is life worth without wine?
>It was created to make people happy.
>>(Ecclesiasticus 31:20,27)

. . . True happiness lies in eating and drinking and enjoying whatever has been achieved under the sun, throughout the life given by God: for this is the lot of humanity. (Ecclesiastes 5:17)

Closing prayer: Bountiful God, I thank you for feeding me and giving me strength. As I marvel at the digestive system, may I also resolve to care for your poor people, who have nothing to eat.

Meditation 13

The Gunpowder Trail: Our Nervous System

Opening prayer: God, who formed us in our mother's womb, may I value my nervous system, without which my body could not act in harmony to build your Reign.

Wondrous Facts

Remember all those old Westerns where the cowboys ran a line of gunpowder along the ground to blow up the wall of a jail cell, a bank vault, or a mine shaft? Our nervous system works a lot like that line of gunpowder particles. A stimulus triggers nerve endings, which ignite the nerve cells next to them, which touch off the next nerve cells, and so on, all the way to the brain. Then *boom*, sensation occurs: "My toes are on fire!" "This is great banana cream pie!"

The nervous system is divided into the central nervous system, consisting of the brain and spinal cord, and the peripheral nervous system, which weaves through every region of the body. The brain will be given separate treatment in meditation 18; this meditation focuses on the rest of the nervous system.

The spinal cord descends from the brain and is protected by the vertebral column. Extending from between the vertebrae are thirty-one pairs of nerves that provide various parts of the body with sensory nerve reception and response, collectively called the peripheral nervous system. Nerves coming off the top portion of the spinal column, for instance, innervate (supply with nerves) the upper parts of the body; nerves branching off the base of the spinal column innervate the lower parts of the body.

Three types of nerve cells, or neurons, are the building blocks of the nervous system. Imagine that you hear a baby crying, for example. Afferent neurons, which transmit "incoming" signals, carry the baby's cry from your ears to the central nervous system. In the central nervous system, interneurons respond by sending a message to the efferent neurons, which transmit "outgoing" signals. Efferent neurons carry the message from the central nervous system, telling your muscles to reach out and pick the baby up.

Suppose again that as you stoop over to lift the baby, the fragrance of fresh-baked apple pie wafts into your nose. Afferent nasal neurons carry this smell sensation to the central nervous system; interneurons "interface" with the brain and signal the efferent neurons to tell the mouth to start salivating and the stomach to crank up secretions. In this whole process, interneurons are the link between afferent and efferent neurons. Interneurons, which comprise about 97 percent of all our nerve cells, also work in the brain to form the connections allowing for memory, emotions, and thought.

Our nervous system contains about twelve billion neurons, around nine billion in the brain and three billion associated with the spinal cord. Some very large neurons transmit signals at three hundred feet per second. At this speed, an average-sized person becomes aware of a stubbed toe in about 3/1000 of a second. Other nerve impulses poke along at only five feet per second.

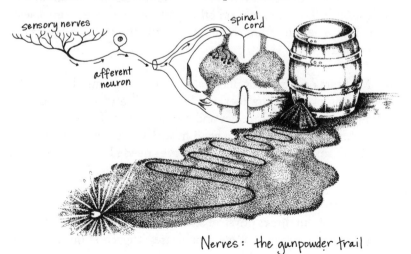

sensory nerves

spinal cord

afferent neuron

Nerves: the gunpowder trail

We are most aware of the part of our nervous system that deals with sensory stimulation and muscular movement—the voluntary nervous system. Working quietly in obscurity, however, is the involuntary (or autonomic) nervous system, which regulates blood pressure, heart rate, digestion, and the secretion of many hormones. The hypothalamus, a small part of the lower forebrain, regulates the autonomic nervous system and such basic drives as thirst and hunger, partially through hormonal control.

Reflection

Prick your finger, and you are immediately aware of it. Hear a melodic flute song, and you become calm. Smell a cologne, and you may remember a date from long ago. All the while, nerves tell your stomach to digest breakfast. The nervous system links our tissues into a whole organism.

🙏 Sit in front of a mirror. Raise your eyebrows. Do they move together? Now swallow. Watch your throat; it should make a bobbing motion. This automatic response moves fluids or solids along down the throat.

🙏 With a wad of cotton or a loosely balled tissue, gently brush your right cheek. Then brush your left cheek. Is the sensation the same? Repeat this gentle brushing on the forehead, on both the right and left sides above the eyebrow. Are the sensations the same? Use this cotton ball or tissue test on other parts of your body—arms, legs, trunk, feet. The sensations should be roughly the same on both sides of your body.

🙏 Meditate on how your nervous system plays a central role in the functioning of your skin, feet and legs, hands and arms, chest and abdomen, sexual organs, bones and muscles, heart, lungs, and digestive system. As you recall the ways in which the nerves work away silently, thank the Creator for the nerves needed by each organ or system.

🙏 We become nervous or stressed from many causes, only some of which come from direct physical stimulation of the nervous system. Our internal nervousness or emotional stress triggers strong reactions in our nervous system, however. Sometimes the system seems to become overloaded, like an electrical transformer that is struck by lightning. Managing stress is one way of nurturing our nervous system.

Draw a picture of what stress feels like to you. The drawing can be an abstract sketch, a symbol, or a cartoon of yourself being stressed out.

&a Do a stress inventory. Brainstorm and write down a list of everything that stresses you. Begin with the stressors that worked on you today, then yesterday, and on back to the last week, month, or even year, writing down the causes of your stress. Make sure that you include in your list *any* conflicts and changes—even positive changes, like a promotion, can cause stress.

On a separate page, list some of the ways in which you most often react to stress, for example, by overeating or becoming moody or physically ill at ease.

Pick out the ten most stressful events from your first list. Then, next to each of these ten stressors, write down the ways in which you managed or relieved the stress connected with it. For example, if you had an argument with a friend, you may have talked through the issue at a later time and patched up the rift.

Next, looking over your lists of stressors and methods of coping with stress, write down your reflections about how you are presently dealing with stress.

Finally, write a dialog with your stress or tension. Let it speak to you, then say something back. Engage in a conversation with your stress.

&a Sometimes a more active way of relieving stress can help. You might try one or both of the following ways, especially if you are angry or frustrated and do not have a direct way of expressing your feelings. (You will probably want to find a room in which you can be alone, undisturbed, and unheard. Because this type of meditation can bring out some strong emotions, you might also want to discuss some of your reactions later with a friend, counselor, or spiritual director.)

- Do you remember how good it felt to stamp your feet when you were angry as a child? Well, try this again. Start by stamping lightly. Gradually move around, stamping with more and more vigor. If it helps, say or even shout something in rhythm.

When you finish stamping, sit down, relax, and breathe deeply. Then spend some time writing to or talking with God about how you felt during the stamping and how you feel now.

◆ Instead of strangling someone, strangle a towel or a small pillow. Exhaust your anger or frustration on this object. Once again, say what's bothering you as you do so. Then, relax, breathe easily, and write to or talk with God about the experience.

✿ Meditating in the presence of God is one of the simplest and most effective ways of reducing strain on the nerves, of reducing stress. Reminding ourself that we live in the embrace of a loving God and then simply being present to God can calm many of our anxieties. Spend some time now recalling God's presence, relaxing your body as you have done in earlier meditations, concentrating on your deep, slow breathing, and perhaps praying a single word like *Love* or *Jesus*.

✿ Leisure, recreation, and play are necessary for nurturing a healthy nervous system. Leisure is a time when a person is free from the demands of work or other duties. Recreation comes, obviously, from re-creating: when we recreate, we build ourself all over. Play is a type of leisure that involves mental or physical exertion but produces no particular outcome other than enjoyment of the activity itself.

Leisure, recreation, or play may come in the form of reading a good novel, swimming laps, knitting, digging a flower bed, or in a hundred other ways. Features that mark an activity as being recreational are as follows: it has no purpose other than enjoyment, it engages you, and it does not seem like work.

In Genesis, God took a whole day off just to enjoy the wonders of Creation. If God needed a day off, human beings probably need two. What about you? Spend some time doing an examen of consciousness about your own "re-creational" life.

◆ Do you have regular physical recreation? If so, describe in writing the effects of this recreation on you. If not, what could you do realistically to recreate yourself physically and mentally?

◆ Recall the ways in which you spend a typical Sunday or day off. List each activity that you might do and the amount of time that you might spend on each one. Then ask yourself and reflect on this question: "What is the quality of my Sunday or day-off leisure?"

* List some energetic leisure activities that require involvement, that you enjoy, but that you have not regularly taken part in. Can you build any of these activities into your schedule?
* Set two goals for yourself about using leisure better, and write them down. Try to be specific and realistic. For instance, "I will go swimming at the YMCA at least three times a week." Then write some specific strategies for meeting your goals, for example, "I will check on a YMCA membership this afternoon."
* Talk with God about your use of leisure and ask for help in meeting your goals for recreation.

God's Word

"You must not set your hearts on things to eat and things to drink; nor must you worry. It is the gentiles of this world who set their hearts on all these things. . . . No; set your hearts on [God's Reign], and these other things will be given you as well.

"There is no need to be afraid, little flock. . . ."(Luke 12:29–32)

Peace I bequeath to you,
my own peace I give you,
a peace which the world cannot give, this is my gift to you.
Do not let your hearts be troubled or afraid.

(John 14:27)

Closing prayer: You have touched me, Jesus. May I always rejoice in the love you have given me. May I be sensitive to the fear and apprehension of my sisters and brothers and bring them peace. May I live always in the calm assurance of your presence.

Meditation 14

Who Knows? Our Nose

Opening prayer: God of all living things, may I rejoice in my nose. It is a source of pleasure and protection. May I have a nose for trouble and for goodness.

Wondrous Facts

The sense of smell is so intricately connected with the associative part of our brain that inhaling some fragrances can have a mood-altering effect. Researchers have found that apple-spice and beach smells produce a calming effect on humans and can actually lower blood pressure.

Taste and smell both contribute to our appreciation of food and drink, but the nose has more power than the tongue when it comes to relishing a curried chicken or a cinnamon roll. A person with a poor sense of smell will usually report an equally poor sense of taste. People need twenty-five thousand times as much of a compound in the mouth to taste it than is needed by scent receptors to smell it. What the brain interprets as taste is often actually smell. When we bite into a sweet strawberry, its fragrance passes up to the nose and tickles our olfactory receptors. Even a strawberry would be next to tasteless if our nose were plugged. A wine taster with a cold is completely out of action.

In general, women have a better sense of smell than do men. The female sex hormone, estrogen, activates the olfactory nerve endings. Musk, a scent associated with male bodies, can be identified by women better than any other odor. In fact, when estrogen levels peak during ovulation, a woman's ability to identify the scent of musk can increase up to one hundred thousand times.

Surprisingly, scents (whether the bouquet of lilac or the stench of sewage) are not identified by the nostrils, but by two small patches of olfactory nerve endings that have a total surface area of less than one square inch. These olfactory patches are located in the roof of the nasal cavities, behind and slightly above the bridge of the nose. The size or shape of the nose plays no real role in the sharpness of the sense of smell. No matter what the size or shape of nose, a person with an acute sense of smell can distinguish approximately ten thousand distinct odors.

The mucous membranes in our nostrils warm, humidify, filter, and ready for identification the airborne molecules we inhale. The identification process remains somewhat of a mystery. It is known that nerve impulses travel to the brain, which then does the sorting. The brain responds in a variety of ways. Some scents cause joy, some cause repulsion, and others trigger fear. Particular scents can also stimulate the hypothalamus and pituitary glands, triggering the release of hormones that control sexual urges, appetite, and body temperature.

Besides smelling, warming, and humidifying inhaled air, another important function performed by the nose is defense against airborne bacteria. A constant flow of mucus and the movement of tiny hairlike cilia carry bacteria to the back of the throat, where they drain into the stomach—and are vanquished by the digestive acids.

Sneezing is another main part of our nasal defense. A hefty sneeze expels large and irritating particles at speeds exceeding one hundred miles per hour.

The nose is directly connected with the part of the brain that recalls and regulates our emotions. For many people, the sense of smell evokes a more intense response than any other sense. The merest hint of an odor can trigger instant, vivid memories of people, places, or events.

Reflection

Imagine not being able to smell! Imagine not having a protective proboscis! No matter how stubby or slender, hooked or pert, our nose knows a lot—the mouth-watering aroma of roasting turkey, the stink of stove gas, the delicate bouquet of sandalwood, and the reek of rotten fish.

Sometimes, perhaps during allergy season or through the course of a wretched cold, we might feel like dispensing with our nose. However, the nose remains a marvel of God's work.

🙠 With your eyes shut, smell the odors around you. See if you can pick out the source of each one. Then go into your kitchen and smell spices, baked goods, fruits, vegetables, and so on. Smell the skin on your arm. Go into your medicine cabinet; open bottles and tubes to smell each one's contents (but be selective—skip the rubbing alcohol). As you do this activity, take your time, savor each fragrance, and thank God for all the various gifts to your nose.

🙠 Go outside. Walk along your street. Take in all the smells. Once again, try to pick out the source of each odor. Pick things up and take a long, appreciative whiff. How long has it been since you picked up some soil and smelled it? What about tree bark or a sun-baked stone?

🙠 Smell can set off vivid memories, whether positive or negative. Recall some instances when smell has brought back memories for you. For instance, maybe the odor of floor wax always causes you to think back to your grade school days.

❧ Our sense of smell protects us from many dangers, like that of leaking gas. Recall times when the gift of smell has protected you from harm; to aid your memory, you might write out your list. Then, make a litany of thanks to the Creator for each time in which your nose has helped you. For example, "My nose picked up the slightly 'high' smell of the chicken at the market. Thank you, gracious God."

❧ Our nostrils are frequently attacked by the stench of pollution. Dialog with the Creator about how you can clean up those parts of the environment, or even very small parts of it, that give off toxic fumes and foul odors.

❧ Meditate on "God's Word" below. How can your life "give off a sweet smell like incense"?

God's Word

Listen to me, devout children, and blossom
    like the rose that grows on the bank of a watercourse.
Give off a sweet smell like incense,
    flower like the lily, spread your fragrance abroad,
sing a song of praise
    blessing [God]. . . .

(Ecclesiasticus 39:13–14)

Closing prayer: Holy God, may I "spread your fragrance abroad" through living a good life. May I make of your earth a garden of sweet smells.

Meditation 15

Camera and Computer: Our Eyes

Opening prayer: Give me sight, Creator God, to see the world as it really is and to see your presence in all of it. All praise to you for the gift of my eyes. Now, help me see.

Wondrous Facts

Almost all living things are sensitive to light. Trees and flowers turn their branches to the sun. Configurations of light entering our eyes tell us what is going on. With our eyes we distinguish the color, relative size and distance of objects, perceive things in three dimensions, and shift focus for near and far vision. While much is known about our eyes, much still remains mysterious.

For example, imagine that you see a wild rabbit in a field of clover. The image on your retina (the "back wall" of your eyeball) is actually fuzzy and jumpy (no pun intended). Between the retina and the brain, the signals become sorted out and sharpened. So when your brain finally says, "Look at the bunny," the image you receive is like that taken by a fine German camera, instead of the fuzzy furball that first hit the retina. This process of sorting out and labeling happens automatically. We do not understand exactly how the eyes work, but they do work marvelously.

Bones of the skull surround the eyes to protect all sides except the fronts, which have lids for this purpose. The eyes rotate in their cavities through the action of orbital muscles. These muscles get the greatest workout of any in the body, moving the eye about one hundred thousand times each day. We would have to walk nearly fifty miles every day to give our legs the equivalent amount of exercise.

Bacteria-fighting fluid secreted by the lacrimal glands constantly cleans and moistens our eyes. The lacrimal glands, located in the lining of the eyelids, increase their secretions in response to irritants such as dust, pollen, or pollution.

Tears caused by irritants are chemically different from tears of sadness. When we cry over a lost love or another emotional upset, our tears contain about 25 percent more of the hormones released by the body during stress periods. These steroid hormones and endorphins are natural painkillers.

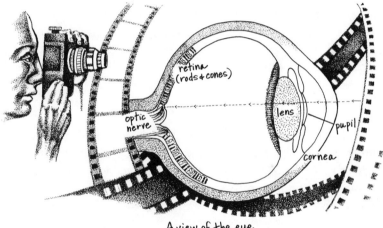

A view of the eye

At the rear of each eyeball, a thick optic nerve links the eye to the visual cortex of the brain, where interpretation of images takes place. To transmit the image of a rose from the front of the eyeball to the visual cortex for identification, light waves must pass through five different tissue layers before the image lands on the retina at the back of the eyeball.

The retina is composed of two types of light-sensitive cells, called rods and cones. The 125 million rods, concentrated around the sides of the retina, process black and white vision at night; the 7 million cones, located mainly in the center of the retina, detect color. Cones are particularly plentiful, and rods absent from, a part of the retina called the fovea. Here, vision is clearest. We also have a literal, though seldom troublesome, "blind spot," where the nerve fibers converge to form the optic nerve, at which there are no rods or cones.

The cones in the retina contain light-sensitive pigments that trigger impulses when certain wavelengths reach them. Cones contain pigments for three basic colors—red, green, and blue. The eye can form a more complete spectrum when it combines the different proportions of the colors being seen.

A deficiency of one or more of the pigment cones in the retina causes color blindness. Most color-blind people cannot distinguish between reds and greens. Rarely will someone suffer blue blindness. Among men, 10 percent experience some color blindness; only 1 percent of women are color-blind.

Finally, eyes age like the other parts of the body. Our lenses harden and thicken throughout life, causing some loss of visual sharpness. Peripheral vision, night vision, and depth perception decrease. At seventy-five years of age, a person's eyes take three times as long to adjust to the dark as those of someone twenty-five.

Reflection

Our eyes need light to see. Healthy eyes depend, however, on open minds in order to see clearly. Sometimes our cynicism or worry can blind us to the light, to the beauty of God's creation. Maybe a way of seeing all of life more fully is to start by marveling at our own eyesight.

🙟 Review the "Wondrous Facts" section in this meditation. Spend time considering one or two of the facts that strike you as marvelous. Consider how these facts have played a role in your life. Then thank God for them.

🙟 If you have not done so recently, give praise to God in one of these ways:
+ If the stars are out, especially if the moon is shining, sit outside and gaze at the night sky. If you have binoculars, put them to use. Relax, breathe deeply, and *see*.
+ Maybe as a child you lay on your back watching the clouds glide overhead. Since a child lives in all of us, go outside to a park—somewhere—and get comfortable. Watch the clouds on parade.

- People-watch. Spend a little time today just seeing people—all of whom are God's creation.
- During a conversation today, maintain eye contact with the other person. Pay close attention to her or him. See, as well as hear, what the person is saying.

❧ The mystic Julian of Norwich once said, "God is everything which is good, as I see, and the goodness which everything has is God" (*Showings*, p. 190). Today, use this statement as a prayer. When you see something particularly marvelous, for example, pray, "God is everything which is good."

❧ Draw some nearby scene. Include as much detail as possible. Leave the drawing for a couple of days. Then take it up again and compare what you drew with the actual scene. Are any significant details of color or shape missing? Is there anything that you just did not see?

❧ Draw a picture of yourself. (You may not be an artist, but give it a try.) Now look at yourself in a mirror. Compare your drawing with the image in the mirror. Did you draw yourself thinner or heavier than you actually are? Taller or shorter? More angular or more rounded? Then ask yourself and talk to God about this question: "Do I see myself as I really am, or is the me in my mind the product of things about myself to which I am blind?" Seeing is not only a matter of having healthy eyes, but having an open mind and heart as well.

❧ Take a camera—you don't even need film—and wander around your house, a park, your neighborhood, looking through the viewfinder. Concentrate on the colors, shapes, movement, and position of the things you see. Really see what is there. Then, dialog with Jesus about this question: Isn't so much of life "as pretty as a postcard" if we only know how to see?

❧ Write and pray a psalm of praise to God for the gift of sight and all the wonders sight allows you to enjoy.

❧ Examine your consciousness on this question: "How have I used the gift of sight to build the Reign of God?"

God's Word

Do not repulse a hard-pressed beggar,
　　nor turn your face from the poor.
Do not avert your eyes from the needy
　　give no one occasion to curse you.

(Ecclesiasticus 4:4–5)

Then turning to his disciples [Jesus] spoke to them by themselves, "Blessed are the eyes that see what you see, for I tell you that many prophets and kings wanted to see what you see, and never saw it. . . ." (Luke 10:23–24)

Closing prayer: Through faith, I see you, Jesus, and believe. May I also see your presence in all of creation, especially in those people in need.

Meditation 16

The Sound and the Swing: Our Ears

Opening prayer: God, you gave us ears to hear your word, whether in a soft breeze or in roaring thunder, in silence or in spoken friendship. Open my ears. Thank you for the gift of hearing.

Wondrous Facts

Our ears are not just for hearing. We also need them in order to keep our balance. Both of these complex functions are camouflaged by the innocuous-looking external ear, which consists simply of the pinna (the large cartilaginous outer part), the lobe, and the auditory canal. Our external ear does little to amplify sound or increase the accuracy of our hearing. Unlike the ears of dogs and many other animals, which can turn independently of the head to home in on sounds, ours cannot even move in the direction of sounds (although some people can wiggle their ears).

The real work of hearing starts in the middle ear, which begins at the membrane known as the eardrum. When, for instance, the notes from a flute hit our eardrum, our eardrum translates these sound waves into unique and distinct vibrations, which are passed along to three tiny bones: the hammer, the anvil, and the stirrup. These bones pick up the eardrum's vibrations, amplify them, and cause the oval window (another membrane) in the inner ear to start vibrating.

The sound waves from the flute now pass into our inner ear. When the oval window vibrates, the fluid in the cochlea (a snail-shaped, fluid-filled organ) begins to vibrate. The actual receptors for acoustic stimulation are approximately twenty-five thousand hairlike projections on a membrane within the cochlea, called the organ of Corti. This organ converts the vibrations into nerve impulses, which are rushed to our brain along the thirty thousand auditory nerve fibers.

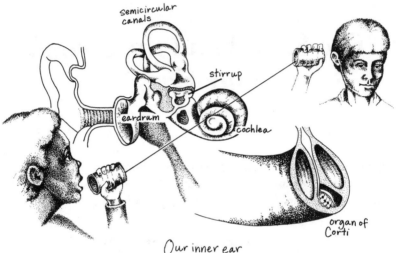

Our inner ear

In order to make sense of these impulses, to identify them as sounds of a flute and not those of a trumpeting elephant, our brain relies on the stored memories of previously heard flute music. Storing sound memories begins at birth. By adulthood we are probably able to distinguish the origin of nearly five hundred thousand different signals.

Sound is measured in decibels. A barely audible whisper measures about 10 decibels. From a hundred feet away, the noise of a jet taking off can hit 130 decibels. Sounds over 100 decibels hurt our ears and may cause hearing loss with prolonged exposure. But then, noise affects just about everyone. Fetuses exposed to environments thick with noise develop more slowly in the womb and weigh less at birth. Here's a handy rule of thumb to determine the level of noise pollution: if you have to raise your voice to be heard, the background noise is too loud and should be avoided.

Most of us can hear high-pitched sounds better than we hear low ones, which might explain why choral directors are usually telling the sopranos or tenors to sing more softly. However, as we age, our ability to hear high-pitched sounds decreases.

The eustachian tube, another resident of our middle ear, connects the middle ear to the back of our throat and provides an exchange of air to the middle ear by opening briefly during swallowing. To equalize the pressure in our ears while going up a mountain, a quick swallow often does the trick.

Our inner ear, with its thousands of auditory nerves, contains no blood vessels because the sound of our own pulse would be deafening. The other sounds of our body—the gurgles of digestion and the wheezes of breathing—are so low that they cannot be heard without the aid of a stethoscope, unless our body is working overtime or in a diseased condition.

One last marvel of the inner ear is its control of our balance. Three fluid-filled, U-shaped tubes (the semicircular canals) located at right angles to each other are set in motion when we move. Hairs next to each tube sense movement and send signals to our brain, which then adjusts our balance. Sometimes even this finely wrought system can be overridden. As a child, did you ever spin around so long and so fast that you actually fell down?

Reflection

With our ears we hear praise and encouragement, abuse and anger. We also hear with our ears the word of God—the words of love—spoken by Jesus and by the people of God around us. Hearing God's word keeps us in balance.

✿ Review the "Wondrous Facts" about our ears. Meditate on one or two especially important facts. How have these particular capabilities been significant in your life?

✿ As you have done before in these meditations, systematically relax your whole body by tensing and relaxing your muscles. . . . Breathe deeply and slowly. . . .

Now, close your eyes for a moment and listen. . . . Pick out each sound, whether loud or soft, far or near. . . . Eventually, just let the sounds mingle together, like the sounds of an orchestra do. . . .

Ponder what it means for you to be able to hear all these sounds. . . . What do you feel? . . . Express your feelings to God. . . .

Finally, offer each sound to God and praise God for allowing you to hear each sound. . . .

𝒫 After you have relaxed your body and closed your eyes, listen to a favorite song or piece of music. Let the sounds sweep over you. If you have never praised God for being able to hear music, do so now by humming, whistling, or singing a hymn of praise.

𝒫 Find the most silent place available. Once you have fully relaxed, listen to your body's sounds. Imagine what the sounds mean, and thank God for the life within your body.

𝒫 Try to recall one or two instances when some sound triggered your memory of an important event or a significant person.

𝒫 Have you heard any affirmations of yourself in the last couple of days? Reflect on this question. Bring to mind any people who have told you positive things or shared their wisdom or stories with you. Thank God for the ability to listen to other people, and pray for each person.

𝒫 Have you been an active listener to anyone? Listening is a blessing for someone who needs to share. Recall how you have given the gift of listening. Thank God for being a listener and ask for open ears, mind, and heart.

𝒫 Psalm 34:6 says, "The poor called; Yahweh heard / and saved them out of all their troubles." How have you inclined your ears to the poor or the needy? Dialog with God about keeping your ears open to "all their troubles."

𝒫 Noise can be a form of pollution, too. Some noises do irreparable damage to creation, especially to our ears. Also, noise causes stress. Ponder the noise in your environment at home, at work, and elsewhere. Are any of the noises damaging to either your emotions or your ears? Consider some practical strategies to counteract the noise pollution in your life.

🍂 Spin, swing, dance, do a cartwheel, or stand on your head: get a little dizzy. Offer this childlike moment to God, in whose loving presence we are all children.

🍂 Hop on a bicycle; go for a ride. Or strap on some skates or roller blades, and go for a skate. As you move along, note all the second-by-second adjustments of balance made by your body automatically. Thank God for your marvelous inner ear.

God's Word

The heart of the intelligent acquires learning,
    the ears of the wise search for knowledge.

(Proverbs 18:15)

"And some seed fell into good soil and grew and produced its crop a hundredfold." Saying this [Jesus] cried, "Anyone who has ears for listening should listen!"
". . . The seed is the word of God." (Luke 8:8,11)

Closing prayer: I have ears, Jesus! Help me to listen to your words. Open my ears, open them. Amen. Alleluia!

Meditation 17

Chat and Chew: Our Mouth

Opening prayer: With my voice, I praise you, God of all goodness. May I revel in the taste of the good things you provide and thank you in song.

Wondrous Facts

Our mouth serves us in many ways. Our tongue tastes (remember the nine thousand taste buds discussed in meditation 12) and helps form distinct sounds. Our teeth chop and grind food. Our voice box produces speech and song, our salivary glands moisten and help clean the mouth cavity, and our tonsils protect us from many harmful bacteria.

The teeth are probably on a par with the tongue as being the most obvious feature of our mouth. Most of us have somewhere between twenty-eight and thirty-two permanent teeth. These grinders, cutters, and mixers move because of powerful muscles in our jaw. These muscles can clamp down with a force of fifty to two hundred pounds per square inch. When the two rows of teeth chomp together as they should—when occlusion is proper—even the smallest bit of rice or carrot or bean will be ground to digestible pulp. If you have ever encountered a small piece of bone or a grain of sand in the food you were chewing, it probably felt like a boulder because of the tight fit between the rows of teeth.

The teeth provide a wonderful example of the way God has built adaptability into the human species. We produce two sets of teeth. Recall your baby teeth. We had twenty of them that started growing at seven months of age and were gone, in most cases, by late childhood. These teeth, also called "milk teeth," have to be replaced for two reasons: first, when we nurse, the strong sugar of the milk easily rots teeth; second, as our mouth grows, baby teeth just would not fill either the space in our mouth or the advanced chewing needs of our adult body. Baby teeth could hardly slice and grind rare meat, for example.

The adult mouth often contains eight incisors, four canines, eight premolars (also called bicuspids), eight molars, and four wisdom teeth. Not all people possess wisdom teeth. It seems that the jaws of humans are smaller than they were ages ago, so many modern mouths cannot accommodate wisdom teeth, which are actually just more molars.

The swallowing reflex provides another great example of adaptability. Let's imagine that you have nibbled (with your incisors) and ground up (with your molars) a raw carrot, and the pulp must make its way to your digestive system. When it gets to the back of your throat, the carrot needs to go to your esophagus—but why doesn't it head down the trachea to the lungs?

The answer is that a series of automatic, muscular movements prevents this from happening, in part by closing off the nasal cavity in the back of your throat. The vocal cords in your larynx also slam shut, and a protective cartilaginous flap, called the epiglottis, swings back to cover the trachea. The opening to your esophagus relaxes and the carrot slides down where it belongs. Occasionally our muscular signals get crossed, allowing food past the trachea, causing choking or possibly infecting the lungs (a good reason to learn the Heimlich maneuver).

The larynx, or voice box, resides in the throat between the upper air passages, the nose, and the lungs. The larynx uses exhaled air to produce sound. (Try speaking while you inhale.) During exhalation, air passes between our vocal cords, causing them to vibrate. Muscles in the throat control these cords, which are semi-hard cartilage. Tight cords narrow the opening and produce high-pitched sound. Loosely vibrating cords produce low tones. The faster the air is forced past the vocal cords, the louder the sound. Our voice takes on its unique character and tone because of the shape and size of our mouth, nose, sinus, throat, and chest cavities. Our voice becomes distorted during a bad cold because these cavities fill with fluid.

The voice box

Speech and diction are further modified by the use of teeth and lips. Forceful emission of air, firmly cut off by our teeth and lips, produces crisp, clear diction. Mumblers have lazy lips.

Our mouth protects us, too. Ready to attack and destroy invading bacteria, two tonsils, packed with lymphocytes (white blood cells), stand guard at the entrance to our throat. We get tonsillitis when our tonsils over-respond to foreign invaders and become inflamed. Saliva also contains antibodies and enzymes that digest bacteria. So our mouth not only allows us to enjoy food and drink and to produce mellifluous sound but is also our first line of defense against airborne and ingested bacteria.

Reflection

Our mouth may speak wisdom or foolishness, sing beautifully or off-key, taste acutely or dully, but it serves the human spirit and body in amazing ways.

𝒫𝒶 Sing your favorite hymn or song. Let your song of praise soar to God as you rejoice in the gifts of speech, language, and song.

🌠 Take a moment to list all the kind words, supportive words, hopeful words, that you spoke today. Next to each word, write the name of the person to whom the word was spoken. Then, by each name, write down why the person needed these words. Finally, lift up the names of these people to God, pray for each person, and thank God for your ability to speak.

Make the same type of inventory for all the kind, supportive, and hopeful words that other people have spoken to you. Thank God for the speech of these companions.

🌠 A simple smile tells other people that we are pleased. A smile on our face also reminds us that life can be good. Today—maybe even all this week—try to smile once or twice more than usual. Do you feel better? Does an extra smile or two help other people?

🌠 Slowly eat one or two of your absolutely favorite foods. Eat deliberately, relishing each mouthful. Enjoy biting, chewing, and swallowing. Pause between bites. Eating slowly like this is not only good for digestion, it also allows you to make eating an experience of appreciating God's bounty.

Now might be the time to taste some foods or beverages that you have always wanted to taste. Experiment; treat your taste buds to something new. Then pause to praise God for prompting our survival and adding to our pleasure by giving us tasting tongues.

🌠 Much like the sense of smell, the sense of taste acts to protect us from tainted food and beverages. Can you remember times when your gift of taste warned you to avoid bad food or drink? As you recall times, thank God for the gift of taste.

🌠 Review the care you take of your teeth. Do you floss and brush properly? Recall the results of your last visit to the dentist. What sort of condition are your teeth in? Do you need to make any changes in your dental stewardship?

🌠 Pray repeatedly out loud the name of Jesus. Pray it using different tones and pitches. Notice how the sound itself evokes different feelings. Find the right tone and pitch and stay with it as you pray Jesus' name.

God's Word

The mouths of the just utter wisdom,
and their tongues speak justice.
The law of God is in their hearts;
their steps do not slip.

(Psalm 37:30–31)

I promise that, ever hopeful,
I will praise you more and more.
My lips shall declare your justice
and power to save, all day long.
I will speak of the works of Yahweh,
commemorate your justice, yours alone.

(Psalm 71:14–16)

Closing prayer: May I utter wisdom and speak justly; and along the way, may I praise you, Creator, by enjoying the wonderful tastes of the earth's harvest.

Meditation 18

Data and Dreams: Our Brain

Opening prayer: Holy Wisdom, what a wonder you made in our brain! Grant me the wisdom to cherish the incredible capacities of my brain.

Wondrous Facts

Protected by the bony skull, our brain is a tightly packed mass of nerve tissue, weighing approximately three pounds. While our brain makes up only 2 percent of our body's total weight, it uses 20 percent of the body's oxygen and blood. Nerve connections located within the brain monitor and control nearly every aspect of bodily function, from moving the smallest toe to calculating the price of a new car to playing Mozart on the piano.

The brain has long been the focus of research but remains largely a mystery. Because of its surrounding skull, the brain is far harder to study than other parts of the body. The mystery and awe with which we regard the brain can be seen in our attitude toward brain surgery. The brain tissue itself, lacking pain receptors, cannot "feel" damage or pain; however, the very thought of brain surgery can send chills up the spines of the strongest people. After all, the brain is the center of life. What if something went wrong during surgery?

Our brain is divided into two hemispheres, the right and the left, both of which are covered by a layer of nerve cells called the cerebral cortex. This cortex receives messages from sensory receptors throughout our body, messages that are relayed through a part of the brain known as the thalamus. Different parts of the cortex specialize in communicating with different parts of the body, for example, with the eyes, ears, mouth, or skin. Outgoing messages from the cortex affect our bodily movement. Some impulses travel at a speed of nearly three hundred feet per second. So when you put your hand on a hot stove, the message from your hand zips to the brain and back to the muscles much faster than a blink of the eyes.

Below the cortex lies the cerebrum, which takes up most of the area of our brain. The cerebrum is the seat of intelligence. All memories reside here. Indeed, up to one hundred billion bits of information can be retained in our memory bank, which is composed of one hundred billion neurons and their one hundred trillion connections.

The thalamus acts as a relay station for sensory data. Surrounding the thalamus, the limbic structure regulates emotional responses. The brain stem monitors our body's ability to be stimulated and houses the control centers for such functions as breathing and swallowing; brain stem injuries usually mean death or permanent coma. The cerebellum smooths out and balances muscular movements, allowing, for example, the coordinated movements needed in ballet dancing or even in threading a needle.

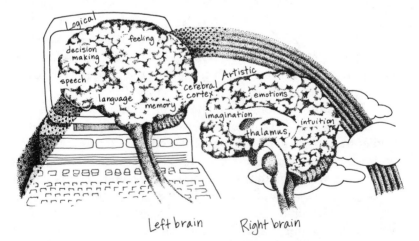

Left brain   Right brain

Although the two hemispheres of the brain may look alike, they actually perform different functions. Because nerve impulses cross to the opposite side of the body before entering the spinal cord, the right hemisphere controls the left side of the body and the left hemisphere controls the right side of the body.

The left side of the brain, often referred to as our "logical" brain, produces language, computes, and undertakes analytical thinking. The person who has only a functioning left hemisphere can describe feelings and sensations, but cannot draw shapes or make music.

The right hemisphere, sometimes called our "artistic" brain, co-ordinates visio-spatial skills and musical talent. Our right brain integrates input from the senses—for example, interpreting body language. The right hemisphere is the seat of our intuition, imagination, and emotion. A person with severe right brain injury will seem to be completely unaware of it; at least, such injury will not cause worry or depression.

Our brain, of all the organs of the body, requires sleep. It requires sleep because, for reasons not completely understood, we need to dream. Indeed, people who have not been allowed to dream for several days will show signs of mental disturbance. Even if we do not remember dreaming, we dream every night. About two hours of an average night's sleep is spent in dream sleep, also known as REM (Rapid Eye Movement) sleep. If something wakes us in the middle of REM sleep, we will recall our dream. Although much remains to be learned about dreams, they seem to allow our subconscious to release its worries and fears. For this reason, sleep, and therefore dream, deprivation can have dire consequences on our mental health. So we should always wish each other sweet dreams—or, at least, dreams.

Reflection

Humans do not have the largest brains of all the animals, either in total weight or in percentage of their body weight. However, the wonders produced by the human brain are staggering. Perhaps most staggering of all is the fact that we are conscious of our own consciousness.

彩 Review the "Wondrous Facts" about the brain. Reflect on facts that you find new and especially marvelous. Talk with Jesus about how these aspects of the brain play an important role in your life.

❧ Have you developed both sides of your brain? Do you employ both logic and intuition? Do you organize data and become enthralled by art? To use both sides of your brain to meditate, try the following:

+ Write a list of all the ways in which you used the left (or "logical") side of your brain today.
+ Now write a list of the times in which you used the right (or "artistic") side of your brain today.

Compare the two lists and answer these questions: "Given the two lists, which side of my brain do I depend on more? Could I develop the less-used side of my brain more fully? If so, how?"

❧ Begin this guided meditation by closing your eyes, breathing deeply, and relaxing your whole body.

You are sitting on a park bench. The sun shines with pleasant warmth, and a fragrant breeze plays across your face. . . . Children fly a brightly painted Chinese-dragon kite that ascends and dips. . . . A mime glides by, on her way to begin a show. . . . You hear the soft melody of a flute somewhere off in the distance. . . . Popcorn pops from a portable popper, and the odor floats your way. . . . Then Jesus walks up and asks to share your bench. . . . Of course, you make room for him. . . .

For a few moments you both sit there in comfortable silence. . . . Finally, Jesus says, "Tell me, what are you thinking?" . . . Collecting your thoughts, you begin telling him about the marvels of your own brain, about learning that has been most valuable, and about what you would like to learn and create in the future. . . .

Jesus says, "Now, my friend, tell me how you are using this wonderful brain of yours to create my Reign here on earth." . . . You reflect on his question, and then you describe ways in which you are using your brain to serve. . . .

Jesus listens with great care. . . . When you are done, he says, "Blessed are those who learn and imagine, solve problems and contemplate mysteries, calculate and create, all for the honor of God and the good of humankind. You are blessed too, my friend." Finally, he stands, embraces you, and walks away. . . .

You spend a few minutes watching the children fly their kite. . . . The mime is climbing stairs now. . . . The popcorn pops once more. . . . Gradually, you come back to the place where you are.

Offer God this meditation. Thank God for the imagination that allows you to consider new combinations of your experience.

♨ Consider these tips, which help foster creativity. As you read each tip, ask yourself how you could use it to develop your own creative ability.

+ Give your intuition and imagination room to function. Creative thought develops best during leisure time that is not crowded or busy.
+ Have a creative space. Creative work requires a definite time and space.
+ Interact with innovative people. Stimulating companions can give a charge to creativity.
+ Ask questions. You can learn a lot from other people by asking open-ended questions about their projects.
+ Break out of ruts. Stretch your imagination by doing things in a way different from usual.
+ Set and keep deadlines for yourself. A deadline helps you get things done and keeps your energies from draining away too easily.
+ Focus your attention and dig deeply. You have to develop a keen relish for learning in your special area of interest.
+ See problems and conflicts as opportunities for creativity. You can be spurred to action by questions and problems.

♨ Review your own patterns of sleep. Are you allowing yourself enough time to dream, time for your mind to renew itself?

God's Word

No, this is the covenant I will make with the House of Israel,
when those days have come, the Lord declares:
In their minds I shall plant my laws
writing them on their hearts.
Then I shall be their God,
and they shall be my people.

(Hebrews 8:10)

Closing prayer: I make my covenant with you, God of the universe, to use my brain to build your Reign.

Meditation 19

Affirming Our Body

Opening prayer: Gracious God, I affirm my body as a wonder of your creation. I cherish who you have made me to be. May I always act with love.

Wondrous Facts

Over eons, the human body has marvelously, slowly undergone minute adaptations that today allow us to breathe, live, and love. Silently, our skin helps regulate the temperature of our body and makes wonderful chemicals to heal our wounds. Two hundred muscles act in harmony to propel us in a single stride. Our human hand has an opposable thumb, useful for grasping elusive shoelaces, tiny pens, and the wiggling fingers of babies. Automatically, seven major muscle groups move together to draw each breath of air. Our sexual organs—male and female—are a wonder of form matching function and serve as a sign that God created us to be creative.

Our bones can stand up to twenty-four thousand pounds per square inch of pressure. Each day our heart pumps nearly two hundred gallons of blood out to the rest of our body. With constant feedback and fine-tuning from the brain, our lungs adjust automatically to provide the eight quarts of air per minute we need when lying down or the fifty quarts per minute we need when running. In one-tenth of a second, our mouth can analyze and identify food. Our nose knows the difference between leaking gas and cooking apples and can trigger waves of powerful memories.

Every moment, thirty thousand auditory nerves rush impulses to our brain, telling us, "Ah, a Haydn flute quartet," or "Terry's in the cookie jar again." Ready to attack and destroy invading bacteria, our lymphocyte-packed tonsils stand guard at the entrance to our throat. Our tongues curl around sounds that whisper of love or sing wild songs. And finally, the brain's trillion cells mysteriously spark and impulse, monitoring and controlling nearly every aspect of our marvelous, magical body.

Reflection

This meditation should help you affirm your body as a whole. Hopefully, by this time, you have realized more fully how wonderful your body is. God would have us see our body for what it is—a gracious gift, made in God's divine image.

In order to bring the process of affirming your body full circle, several of these reflection activities are based on those of the first meditation in this book, "Appraising Our Body Image."

✿ Relax your body by stretching each part. Start with your feet. Stretch and relax. Then your legs, and so on, until you have stretched and relaxed your entire body.

Close your eyes and get in touch with how you are experiencing your body right now. How do you feel about your body? Make a mental tour of your body from top to bottom to inventory your feelings.

When you have finished this "feelings inventory," spend some time writing down your feelings. List them in any order. Then try to write a summary of your feelings.

Now, write your reactions to these questions:
* Are you feeling better, more alive, now that you have spent this time meditating on your body—and if so, in what ways do you feel better?
* How would you *like* to grow in affirming your body?

✿ Slow down. Sit comfortably but alertly. Breathe deeply and slowly for several minutes. Concentrate on your deep breathing, close your eyes, and relax.

Imagine that you are at a party or gathering. Someone whom you admire greatly, and whom you have met once before, is also at this party. This person sees you and comes toward you from across the room. How do you feel about your body in the presence of this person?

Ponder, perhaps in writing, on what your reactions during this meditation exercise say about your body image now.

✸ Position yourself before a mirror, preferably one that allows you to see your entire body. Slowly pray the following litany. As you do, look at the part of your body about which you are praying.

- Gracious God, thank you for the gift of my skin.
- I thank you, Creator God, for my feet and legs.
- For my arms and hands, I give thanks to you, God.
- Source of life and all delight, I thank you for my chest and abdomen.
- Giver of my life, thank you for my sexual organs.
- For bones and muscles, I give you thanks.
- Lungs and heart you have given me. Thank you, good God.
- Creator God, for my digestive system, thanks.
- I give you thanks for my nervous system.
- For my nose, eyes, ears, mouth, and voice, I give you thanks.
- Loving God, thank you for my brain.
- God, you created me in your image and likeness. I give you thanks for the miracle of my body, for all of me.

Conclude your litany-meditation by caressing your body with your eyes. Then, in writing, express your reactions to the litany-meditation in the form of a prayer to God, who created you.

✸ Once again, close your eyes, breathe deeply, and relax your body. Concentrate on your slow, rhythmic breathing for a while.

Now, let's go on a journey. . . . See and feel yourself walking slowly through a clearing in the forest. . . . Tall grass and wildflowers wave in the soft breeze. . . . The sun caresses your face. . . . You stop to take in the scene. . . . Birds flit among the wildflowers and fly into the pine trees ahead of you. . . . Butterflies float among the flowers. . . . One of them stops near you. . . . You hardly breathe so that it won't wing away. . . . You inhale the fragrances carried by the wind. . . . You breathe in and out deeply several times. . . . Slowly you continue to walk toward the forest. . . .

A person sits on a log in the shade. . . . With a slight wave of the hand, the person invites you to share the log as a seat. . . .

When you are close, he says, "Peace be with you." . . . Your eyes are opened, and you know that he is Jesus. . . . You look deeply into his eyes. . . . Jesus reaches out and takes your hand in his and says, "I love you with an everlasting love."

Softly he says to you, "Now, my friend, tell me, do you love yourself as I love you? Have you accepted the wonder of creation that you are? Talk to me about all the goodness that you have discovered in yourself." . . . You pause to gather your feelings and words. . . . Then you tell Jesus all your thoughts and feelings about your body, your joys and sorrows, loves and questions. . . . He listens attentively. . . .

When you have finished speaking, Jesus stands to go, saying, "Because you have loved much, your sins are forgiven. Do not doubt the profound goodness of your own creation, for you are made in my image." . . . He embraces you. . . . While holding you, he whispers, "My desire is that you be healed in spirit." . . . After a long embrace, he releases you and turns, walking slowly into the forest. . . . When he has disappeared, you gaze at the scene around you once more. . . . When you are ready, return from the scene and open your eyes.

God's Word

God said, "Let us make human beings in our own image, in the likeness of ourselves." . . . God created human beings in

God's own image, in the image of God they were created, male and female God created them. . . . God blessed them. . . . And so it was, looking at all of Creation, God recognized it as very good. (Adapted from Genesis 1:26–31)

Closing prayer: I am created in God's image. For the wonder of myself, and for all my sisters and brothers, I thank you, loving God.

Meditation 20

Nurturing Our Body

Opening prayer: All-good God, you created us for health and holiness. Guide me now as I ponder and plan ways of nurturing my body for your glory and the service of the human family.

Wondrous Facts

Most of us probably have favorite stories of people who have decided to make changes in their lifestyle toward greater wellness. Maybe your favorite story is your own. A friend told this story about his conversion to wellness and to a profound respect for his body:

> About ten years ago, I contracted rheumatic fever. I was out camping and woke up in the middle of the night with my leg and hip joints swollen tight. I could barely crawl out of the tent. I spent the next week waiting for tests to tell me whether I had the fever or rheumatoid arthritis, then a couple more weeks waiting to find out how much Swiss cheese the fever had made of my heart.
>
> I escaped unscathed, but I felt that I had let this happen. I had become run-down and out of shape. Looking back, I saw that I spent my twenties squandering my health.
>
> I decided not to live like that anymore, but it has taken most of the last ten years to live up to that decision. My wife is a huge help. We encourage each other to, as we put it, "stay hungry and keep moving." To our delight, we find that this leads to a better, simpler lifestyle—good food is often the

cheapest, and daily exercise can mean hiking through the neighborhood.

Life offers no guarantees. Rheumatic fever can recur or I can keel over tomorrow from something else sudden or dreadful. I just refuse to hand over my health—Death will have to get out of his TV lounger and come get it.

It is a wonderful fact that we have the ability to change some aspects of our body.

We have no power over where we were born or whom we were born to. We are influenced by cosmic occurrences that insurance companies call "acts of God," such as earthquakes and hurricanes; we are influenced by rainbows, and gentle rain. Some of us can wiggle our ears and roll our tongue, and others cannot. Someday we will die. For all this, much of our wellness depends on our decisions.

Maybe the most important influence many of us need to change is the negative environment that surrounds our body. Some of us need courage to heal memories of abuse inflicted by other people, or maybe by ourself. Perhaps we need to change our diet or pattern of exercise.

The Serenity Prayer says:

God, grant me
serenity to accept
the things I cannot change,
courage to change the things I can,
and wisdom to know the difference.

In the last meditation, you had a chance to affirm the fact that your body is a wonderful creation from God. In this meditation, you are invited to accept the things you cannot change about your body, to look at what you want to change, and to seek the courage to change it. Your body is a constantly evolving work of art. You and God are the artists.

Reflection

Now may be the time for us to reflect on the changes that we can make in our lifestyle. We are called to co-create the Reign of God. How can you co-create your body, so that it is as fully alive as it can be? God stands always ready to help in this co-creation.

❧ Listed below are statements that describe good health habits. Consider each one and ask yourself how you are doing in that particular area. If you are satisfied with your achievement, thank God and pray for continued success. If you want to change your behavior, write down a realistic plan of action that would lead you to a healthier way of living. Then pray for God's assistance in sticking to this plan.

- I eat a variety of healthy foods like fruits, vegetables, whole-grain breads and cereals, lean meats, and dairy products.
- I am careful in the amounts of fat, saturated fat, and cholesterol-rich foods that I eat.
- I limit my salt and sugar intake by monitoring my cooking and eating habits.
- I maintain a healthy weight.
- I do some vigorous exercise for fifteen to thirty minutes at least three times each week.
- I take leisure time away from work to recreate myself and develop other interests in life.
- I do not smoke, and I avoid smoke-filled places.
- If I drink alcoholic beverages, I do so moderately and not as a way of handling stress or problems.
- I monitor medications that I take.
- I enjoy and find some meaning in my work.
- I maintain close friendships and good relationships with my family.
- I give appropriate expression to my feelings.
- I avoid, when possible, situations that will cause negative stress.
- I drive safely and wear a seat belt.
- I regularly spend quality time in meditation and prayer.
- I read and try to grow intellectually.

❧ List three positive attitudes that you had about your body in the past. Have these attitudes been maintained or changed as of right now? How could you develop these three positive attitudes even more in the future?

Next, list three negative attitudes that you had in the past about your body. Then describe the status of each of these attitudes right now, and finally, describe attitudes you would like to have in the future.

🙠 Do some dreaming about how you would like to see your body in five years. Then draw a picture of "me in my body five years from now." Dialog with the Creator about your picture.

🙠 Draw up a list of five or six statements that affirm your bodiliness, for example, "Body and spirit, I am a gift from God," or "I am a wonder of creation." Write one or several of these affirmations in fancy lettering and paste them on your bathroom mirror or at different places around your home. Resolve to pray these affirmations several times each day.

🙠 Discuss with God how a sense of wholeness about your body will assist you in building the Reign of God on earth.

God's Word

Do you not realise that you are a temple of God with the Spirit of God living in you? If anybody should destroy the temple of God, God will destroy that person, because God's temple is holy; and you are that temple. (1 Corinthians 3:16–17)

We are God's work of art, created in Christ Jesus for the good works which God has already designated to make up our way of life. (Ephesians 2:10)

Closing prayer:

> You, God, created my inmost being
> and knit me together in my mother's womb.
> For all these mysteries—
> for the wonder of myself,
> for the wonder of your works—
> I thank you.

(Psalm 139:13–14)

Amen. Alleluia!

Appendix

Suggestions for Meditating on Your Body

Create a sacred space. Jesus said, " 'When you pray, go to your private room, shut yourself in, and so pray to [God] who is in that secret place, and [God] who sees all that is done in secret will reward you' " (Matthew 6:6). Solitary prayer is best done in a place where you can have privacy and silence, both of which can be luxuries in the lives of busy people. Try to create a prayerful mood with candles, meditative music, an open Bible, or a crucifix. Wearing loose-fitting, comfortable clothes will be particularly desirable during these prayers.

If privacy and silence are not possible, create a quiet, safe place within yourself, perhaps while riding to or from work, while sitting in line at the dentist's office, or while waiting for someone. Do the best you can, knowing that a loving God is present everywhere.

Open yourself to the power of prayer. Every human experience has a religious dimension. All of life is suffused with God's presence. As you begin your period of prayer, remind yourself that God is present. Do not worry about distractions. If something keeps intruding during your prayer, talk with God about it. Be flexible, because the Spirit of God blows where it will.

Prayer can open your mind and broaden your vision. Be open to new ways of seeing God, other people, and yourself. As you open yourself to the Spirit of God, different emotions will be evoked, such as sadness from tender memories or joy from a celebration recalled. Our emotions are messages from God that can tell us much about our spiritual quest. Also, prayer strengthens our will to act. Through prayer, God can touch our will and empower us to live according to what we know is true.

Finally, many of the meditations in this book will call on you to employ your memory, your imagination, and your life as subjects for prayer. The great mystics and saints realized that they had to use all their resources to know God better. Indeed, God speaks to us continually and touches us constantly. We must learn to listen and feel with all the means that God gives us.

Come to these prayers with an open mind, heart, and will to newly wonder at, value, and delight in the body God gave you.

Preview each meditation before beginning. Spend a few moments previewing the meditation, especially the reflection activities. Several reflection activities are given in each meditation because different styles of prayer appeal to different personalities or personal needs. Select only one or two reflection activities each time you use a meditation. Be sure to gather any necessary materials (for example, a journal and pen, or a mirror) before you begin the actual meditation.

Use the reflections. Following the reading is a short reflection in commentary form, which is meant to give perspective to the reading. Then you will be offered several ways of meditating on the particular aspect of your body that is the subject of the prayer. You may be familiar with the different methods of meditating, but in case you are not, they are described briefly here.

+ *Repeated short prayer:* One means of focusing your prayer is to use a prayer word or a short phrase. For example, a prayer word about our ears might be "Speak, Friend." As you inhale, say silently "Speak," and as you exhale, say "Friend." Repeated slowly in harmony with your breathing, the prayer word helps you bring your body, heart, and mind in harmony with God.

+ *Guided meditation:* In this type of meditation, our imagination helps us consider alternative actions and likely consequences. Our imagination helps us experience new ways of seeing God, our neighbors, our body, and ourself. When Jesus told his followers parables and stories, he engaged their imagination. In this book you will be invited to follow guided meditations.

One way of doing a guided meditation is to read the scene or story several times, until you know the outline and can recall it when you enter into reflection. Or before your prayer time, you may wish to record the meditation on a tape recorder. If so, re-member to allow pauses for reflection between phrases and to speak with a slow, peaceful pace and tone. Then during prayer, when you have finished the reading and the reflection commen-tary, you can turn on your recording of the meditation and be led through it. If you find your own voice too distracting, ask a friend to make the tape for you.

- *Examen of consciousness:* The reflections will often ask you to ex-amine how God has been speaking to you in your past and pre-sent experiences—in other words, the reflections will ask you to examine your awareness of God's presence in your life, especially in relation to your bodiliness.

- *Journal writing:* Writing is a process of discovery. If you write for any length of time, stating honestly what is on your mind and in your heart, you will unearth much about who you are, how you stand with God, what deep longings reside in your soul, and more. In some reflections you will be asked to write a dialog with your body, with Jesus, or with someone else. When doing these, try to put yourself in the position of the body part or the other person: allow yourself to view the world from another perspec-tive. This might seem strange at first, but you may find helpful insights. Try writing the dialog like a play script. For instance, a dialog with your feet might begin like this:
  Feet: I hate the shoes you buy me.
  Me: But I buy good shoes. I spend good money on them. What's wrong?
  Feet: Hard soles. Sure, they look good, but I'm sore from walk-ing on cement.
If you have never used writing as a means of meditation, try it. Reserve a special notebook for your journal writing. If you desire, you can go back to your entries at a future time.

- *Action:* Occasionally, a reflection will suggest some form of phys-ical activity like massaging your feet or hands, flexing your mus-cles, singing a favorite hymn, or going out for a walk. Especially in these meditations, action can be a meaningful form of prayer. If you review a meditation before you begin your prayer period, you can find out if the reflection activities invite some move-ment or other physical action. Thus, you can wear clothes com-fortable for movement.